Classic ——————————

Vegetarian

—————————— Recipes

Classic Vegetarian Recipes

Sue Ashworth

Carole Handslip

Kathryn Hawkins

Cara Hobday

Jenny Stacey

Rosemary Wadey

Pamela Westland

SMITHMARK

This edition published in 1998 by SMITHMARK Publishers,
a division of U.S. Media Holdings Inc.,
115 West 18th Street., New York, NY 10011.

SMITHMARK books are available for bulk purchase for sales promotion and premium
use. For details write or call the manager of special sales, SMITHMARK Publishers,
115 West 18th Street, New York, NY 10011.

Edited, designed, and produced by Haldane Mason, London

Acknowledgements
Editor: Jo-Anne Cox
Editorial Assistant: Elizabeth Towers
Design: dap ltd
Photographers: Karl Adamson, Sue Atkinson, Iain Bagwell, Amanda Heywood,
Joff Lee, Patrick McLeavey, Clive Streeter, Andrew Sydenham
Home Economists: Sue Ashworth, Sue Atkinson, Carole Handslip, Kathryn Hawkins,
Cara Hobday, Louise Pickford, Rosemary Wadey

ISBN: 0–7651–0881–X

Printed in Italy

10 9 8 7 6 5 4 3 2 1

Note
Tablespoons are assumed to be 15 ml. Unless otherwise stated, milk is
assumed to be full-fat, eggs are medium, and pepper is freshly ground black pepper.

Contents

Introduction 8

Soups & Starters 20

Light Meals 60

Pasta Dishes 98

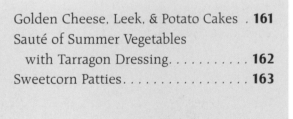

Grains & Legumes 118

Stir-fries & Sautés 144

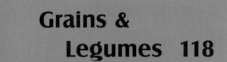

Bakes & Roasts 164

Side Dishes & Salads 190

Desserts 226

Index 252

Introduction

*People choose to eat vegetarian food for all sorts of different reasons, whether on
moral grounds, for health reasons, for economy, or simply because they prefer the flavor.
Whatever the motive, one thing is certain—everyone enjoys good food, and vegetarian food
can be as good as, and indeed often better than, traditional meat and fish dishes.
Vegetarian meals are perfect for entertaining or just for the family to enjoy,
and can be easily adapted to suit all tastes.*

This inspirational cookbook is designed to appeal to vegetarians and vegans alike as it contains a wide range of recipes which will appeal to all. Another aim is to dispel the myth that vegetarian food is brown, stodgy, and bland. When browsing through the recipes you will discover just how versatile, colorful, and flavorful a vegetarian diet can be. It makes perfect sense when you consider the natural foods used and the wide range of produce available all year round, all of which are suitable for the vegetarian diet.

With the advent of refrigerated transport, fresh produce is now shipped from all over the world to give us a whole array of fresh fruit and vegetables with which to create delicious recipes. The use of exotic spices, fresh herbs and garlic, sauces, and relishes makes for an exciting and healthy diet.

Eating a balanced, healthy diet is very important. This can be easily achieved by combining the different recipes in this book when planning your meal, to include protein, carbohydrate, vitamins, minerals, and some fats. It is very important in any diet, but especially a vegetarian diet, that a good balance is achieved and that sufficient protein is eaten, and you should bear this in mind when deciding which of the wonderful recipes to try in the chapters that follow.

When it comes to recipes, there are dishes from far and wide, including the Orient, Middle East, and the Mediterranean. The diets in these regions are healthy and the native ingredients and flavorings are exciting and delicious. The book also contains more familiar recipes and variations on themes, such as Vegetable Toad-in-the-Hole, a quick, tasty family meal in which I guarantee that the meat won't be missed. Indeed, this can be said for all of the recipes in this book. Many could be served to meat-eating guests without them missing the "meat factor" in any way. It is the perfect way to introduce your friends to this healthy and delicious diet.

When cooking the following recipes, feel free to substitute some of the ingredients to suit specific diets, using soya milk, for example, instead of cow's milk, cream substitute instead of the dairy cream, and vegetarian margarine instead of butter. In this way you will enjoy a whole range of super starters, tasty light meals and snacks, wonderful main meals and accompaniments, and delicious desserts. This cookbook will allow you to discover or reaffirm that the vegetarian diet has progressed greatly from the nut cutlet to a colorful and imaginative way of eating. Enjoy!

VEGETARIAN NUTRITION

Vegetarian food is extremely healthy, and can provide all the important vitamins, minerals, proteins, carbohydrates, and fats that make up a nutritious, well-balanced diet. And because more fruit, vegetables, grains, and legumes tend to be eaten, the diet is rich in complex carbohydrates, the primary source of energy and fiber, which helps to keep the body vibrant and healthy.

Protein

Obtaining sufficient protein is not a problem in a vegetarian diet as there are plenty of foods from which to choose. Eggs, cheese, milk, nuts, beans, and soya products, such as texturized vegetable protein, soya milk, bean curd, Quorn or mycoprotein, are all excellent sources. Make sure that you eat a wide variety of these foods to get the full range of protein that your body needs.

Fat

Another additional benefit of following a vegetarian diet is that it can be quite low in fat. The main sources of fat in your diet will be from vegetable, nut and olive oils, dairy foods, nuts, and any products containing these ingredients. So dieters can succeed in losing weight following a vegetarian diet, provided they keep an eye on their overall fat intake.

Carbohydrates

A vegetarian diet is rich in complex carbohydrates, found in starchy foods, such as brown rice, oats, and whole wheat pasta and bread. These are particularly useful to dieters, as they ensure a steady release of energy and a stable blood sugar level.

Vitamins

Fruit and vegetables are packed with important vitamins, essential for our general well-being and the healthy functioning of our bodies. If you follow a vegetarian diet, you can't go wrong.

The best sources of vitamin A are yellow fruits and vegetables and some green vegetables—apricots, peaches, spinach, and carrots, for example. It is also present in butter and added to margarines. Vitamin A helps us to resist infections and keeps the skin, hair, eyes, and body tissues in healthy condition.

The B group vitamins act as a catalyst in the releasing of energy from food. They are also vital for the maintenance of a healthy nervous system and red blood cells. Apart from vitamin B12, all the B vitamins can be found in yeast and wholegrain cereals, especially wheat flour and wheatgerm. Vegetarians eating a wide variety of foods should therefore have no problem in obtaining enough B vitamins, although vegans (who do not eat dairy products) need to include some sort of B12 supplement in their diet.

Vitamin C is well-known for helping to prevent infections

and is firmly believed by many to assist in warding off, as well as curing, winter colds and 'flu. Eat foods rich in vitamin C with iron-rich foods, as it helps to increase the absorption of iron. Fresh fruit, leafy vegetables, tomatoes, bell peppers, and potatoes are all good sources. Avoid drinking tea, coffee, and certain soft drinks with foods that contain vitamin C, as the caffeine can actually decrease the amount of vitamin C your body subsequently absorbs. Since vitamin C is easily destroyed during cooking, only use a small amount of water when boiling vegetables to cook them as quickly as possible. This will minimize the risk of the vitamin leaking into the cooking water.

The other important vitamin for good health is vitamin D, which enables the body to absorb calcium, thus providing strong bones and teeth. Vitamin D is often known as the "sunshine vitamin", as the body can manufacture its own supply from exposure to sunlight. Good food sources include eggs, cheese, margarine, and butter.

Minerals

Minerals are another group of vital nutrients that are needed by the human body. Although only minute amounts are required, minerals need to be supplied on a regular basis. It makes sense to get to know which foods contain them, and make sure you are getting plenty of these in your diet. There should be no problem as long as you eat a wide variety of foods.

Calcium is found in milk, cheese, yogurt and other dairy products, leafy green vegetables, bread, nuts, seeds, and dried fruits. Iron is found in beans, seeds, nuts, eggs, cocoa powder, chocolate, whole wheat bread, leafy green vegetables, and dried fruits (especially apricots and figs). Other important minerals include magnesium, phosphorus, potassium and zinc.

THE VEGETARIAN SHOPPING BASKET

When shopping for vegetarian foods, make sure that you are not buying animal products unawares. Choose cheese that is made from vegetarian rennet; buy agar-agar or gelozone instead of gelatine; select a vegetarian suet instead of beef suet—no, you won't have to forego delicious dumplings!

Be aware of what you are spreading on your bread too. Some margarines are not suitable as they contain both fish oils and animal fats, so check that you are buying a brand made entirely of vegetable oil. Butter is perfect, unless, of course, you are a vegan.

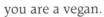

The Vegetarian Cupboard

A well-stocked cupboard forms the backbone of any good cook's kitchen, and it is always useful to have plenty of basic foods ready to hand. Use the following information as a checklist when you need to replenish your stocks.

Flour

You will need to keep a selection of flours: all-purpose and self-rising flour if you want to make your own bread, and whole wheat flour, either for using on its own or for combining with white flour for cakes and pastries. You may also like to keep some rice flour and cornstarch for thickening sauces and to add to cakes, biscuits, and puddings. Buckwheat, garbanzo bean, and soya flours can also be bought. These are useful for pancakes and for combining with other flours in order to add different flavors and textures.

Grains

A good variety of grains is essential. For rice, choose from long-grain, basmati, Italian arborio for making risotto, short-grain for puddings, and wild rice to add flavor and interest. Look out for fragrant Thai rice, jasmine rice and combinations of different varieties to add color and texture to your dishes. When choosing your rice, remember that brown rice is a much better source of vitamin B1 and fiber.

Other grains add variety to the diet. Try to include some barley (whole grain or pearl), millet, bulgar wheat, polenta (made from maize), oats (oatmeal, oatflakes, or oatbran), semolina —including cous-cous (from which it is made), sago, and tapioca.

Pasta

Pasta has become much more popular recently, and there are many types and shapes to choose from. Keep a good selection, and always make sure you have the basic lasagne sheets, tagliatelle or fettuccine (flat ribbons), and spaghetti. Try spinach- or tomato-flavored varieties for a change, and sample some of the many fresh pastas now available. Better still, make your own—handrolling pasta, while undoubtedly time-consuming, can be very satisfying, but you can buy a special machine for rolling the dough and cutting certain shapes. You could also buy a wooden "pasta tree" on which to hang the pasta to dry, in which case you might find you get enthusiastic help, especially if you have small children!

Legumes

Legumes are very important in a vegetarian diet as they are a valuable source of protein, vitamins, and minerals. Stock up on soya beans, navy beans, red kidney beans, cannellini beans, garbanzo beans, all types of lentils, split peas, and butter beans. Buy dried legumes for soaking and cooking yourself, or canned varieties for speed and convenience.

It is important to cook dried red and black kidney beans in plenty of vigorously boiling water for 15 minutes to destroy harmful toxins in the outer skin. Drain and rinse the beans, and then continue to simmer until the beans are tender. Soya beans should be boiled for 1 hour, as they contain a substance that inhibits protein absorption.

Spices and Herbs

A good selection of spices and herbs is important for adding variety and interest to your cooking—add to your range each time you try a new recipe. There are some good spice mixtures available—try Cajun, Chinese five-spice powder, Indonesian piri-piri, and the different curry blends. Try grinding your own spices with a mortar and pestle, or in a coffee mill (wash well after using!), to make your own blends, or just experiment with those that you can buy. Although spices will keep well, don't leave them in the cupboard for too long, as they may lose some of their strength. Buy small amounts as you need them.

Fresh herbs are always preferable to dried, but it is essential to have dried ones in stock as a useful back-up. Keep the basics such as thyme, rosemary, bay leaves, and some good Mediterranean mixtures for Italian and French cooking.

Chilies

These come both fresh and dried and in colors from green through yellow, orange, and red to brown. The "hotness" varies so use with caution, but as a guide the smaller they are the hotter they will be. The seeds are hottest and are usually discarded. When cutting chilies with bare hands do not touch your eyes; the juices will cause severe irritation.

Chili powder should also be used sparingly. Check whether the powder is pure chili or a chili seasoning or blend, which should be milder. Chili sauces are also used widely in oriental cookery, but again they vary in strength from hot to exceedingly hot, as well as in sweetness.

Nuts and Seeds

As well as adding protein, vitamins, and useful fats to the diet, nuts and seeds add important flavor and texture to vegetarian meals. To bring out the flavor of nuts and seeds, broil or roast them until lightly browned.

Make sure that you keep a good supply of almonds, brazils, cashews, chestnuts (dried or canned), hazelnuts, peanuts, pecans, pine nuts, pistachios, and walnuts. Coconut—either creamed or shredded—is useful too.

For your seed collection, sesame, sunflower, pumpkin, and poppy seeds are a good choice. Pumpkin seeds in particular are an excellent source of zinc.

Dried Fruits

Currants, raisins, golden raisins, dates, apples, apricots, figs, pears, peaches, prunes, papayas, mangoes, figs, bananas, and pineapples can all be purchased dried and can be used in lots of different recipes. When buying dried fruits, look for untreated varieties: for example, buy figs that have not been rolled in sugar, and choose unsulphured apricots, if they are available.

Although dried fruits are a healthier alternative to cookies and candies, they are still high in calories, being a natural source of sugar.

Oils and Fats

Oils are useful for adding subtle flavorings to foods, so it is a good idea to have a selection in your cupboard. Use a light olive oil for cooking and extra-virgin olive oil for salad dressings. Use sunflower oil as a good general-purpose oil and select one or two specialty oils to add character to different dishes. Sesame oil is wonderful in stir-fries; hazelnut and walnut oils are superb in salad dressings.

Oils and fats add flavor to foods, and contain the important fat-soluble vitamins A, D, E, and K. Remember all fats and oils are high in calories, and that oils are higher in calories than butter or margarine—one tablespoon of oil contains 134 calories, whereas one tablespoon of butter or margarine contains 110 calories. When you are using oil in dressings or adding it to a wok or skillet, it is a good idea to measure it—it's easy to use twice as much oil without fully realizing.

Vinegars

Choose three or four vinegars—red or white wine, cider, light malt, tarragon, sherry, or balsamic vinegar, to name just a few. Each will add its own character to your recipes.

Mustards

Mustards are made from black, brown, or white mustard seeds which are ground, mixed with spices and then, usually, mixed with vinegar.

Meaux mustard is made from mixed mustard seeds and has a grainy texture with a warm, spicy taste.

Dijon mustard, made from husked and ground mustard seeds, is medium-hot and has a sharp flavor. Its versatility in salads and with barbecues makes it an ideal mustard for the vegetarian. It is made in Dijon, France, and only mustard made there can be labelled as such.

German mustard is mild sweet/sour and is best used in Scandinavian and German dishes.

Bottled Sauces

Soy sauce is widely used in all Eastern cookery and is made from fermented yellow soya beans mixed with wheat, salt, yeast, and sugar. It comes in both light and dark varieties. Light soy sauce tends to be rather salty, whereas dark soy sauce tends to be sweeter and is more often used in dips and sauces.

Teriyaki sauce gives an authentic Japanese flavoring to stir-fries. Thick and dark brown, it contains soy sauce, vinegar, sesame oil, and spices as main ingredients.

Black bean and yellow bean sauces add an instant authentic Chinese flavor to stir-fries. Black bean sauce is the stronger; the yellow bean variety is milder and is excellent with vegetables.

USEFUL EXTRAS

Sesame seed paste, yeast extract, sea salt, black and green peppercorns, tomato and garlic pastes, vegetable bouillon cubes, dried yeast, gelozone, or agar-agar are all useful cupboard additions.

THE VEGETARIAN FRIDGE AND FREEZER

Thankfully, food manufacturers have wised up to the fact that lots of us love to eat vegetarian food, so it is now possible to choose from a huge range of prepared meals from the chilled or frozen food cabinets. These are excellent standbys for when you want a meal in a hurry, and they add variety and choice to the diet. Pasta dishes, vegetable bakes and burgers, curries, flans, and quiches are just some of the dishes to choose from.

Besides stocking a selection of ready-made meals, freeze other basics such as frozen pastries (shortcrust, filo, or puff pastry); a selection of breads, such as pita, French bread, rolls or part-baked bread; pre-cooked pasta dishes, pasta sauces, vegetable stock, bread crumbs, homemade soups and sauces, flan cases, pancakes, pizza bases, and so on. All these will be useful when you are short of time.

THE SECRET OF SUCCESS

As with any cooking, the choice of ingredients is of paramount importance. If they are fresh and of good quality, you are well on your way to achieving delicious food. Not only will the flavors be better, but so will the colors, textures, and nutritious value. Fresh fruit and vegetables lose their vitamin content very quickly if stored for too long, so buy from the freshest possible source, and use soon after buying.

Basic Recipes

Vegetarian stocks and sauces are invaluable for many recipes. Here are a few basics.

Fresh Vegetable Stock

This can be kept chilled for up to three days or frozen for up to three months. Salt is not added when cooking the stock: it is better to season it according to the dish in which it is to be used. Makes 6¼ cups.

9 ounces shallots
1 large carrot, diced
1 celery stalk, chopped
½ fennel bulb
1 garlic clove
1 bay leaf
a few fresh parsley and tarragon sprigs
8¾ cups water
pepper

1 Put all the ingredients in a large saucepan and bring to a boil. Skim off the surface scum with a flat spoon and reduce to a gentle simmer. Partially cover and cook for 45 minutes. Leave to cool.

2 Line a strainer with clean cheesecloth and put over a large jug or bowl. Pour the stock through the strainer. Discard the herbs and vegetables. Cover and store in small quantities in the refrigerator for up to three days.

Tahini Cream

Tahini is a paste made from sesame seeds. This nutty-flavored sauce is good served with Kofta Kabobs (see page 135) and other Middle Eastern dishes, such as Falafel (see page 76). Makes ⅔ cup.

3 tbsp sesame seed paste
6 tbsp water
2 tsp lemon juice
1 garlic clove, crushed
salt and pepper

1 Blend together the sesame seed paste and water. Stir in the lemon juice and garlic. Season with salt and freshly ground black pepper.

Béchamel Sauce

This basic white sauce can be used in all kinds of dishes. Flavor it with grated cheese or chopped fresh herbs if you like. Makes 2½ cups.

2½ cups milk
4 cloves
1 bay leaf
pinch of freshly grated nutmeg
2 tbsp butter or vegetarian margarine
¼ cup all-purpose flour
salt and pepper

1 Put the milk in a saucepan and add the cloves, bay leaf, and nutmeg. Gradually bring to a boil. Remove from the heat and leave for 15 minutes.

2 Melt the butter or margarine in another saucepan and stir in the flour to form a roux. Cook, stirring, for 1 minute.

3 Remove from the heat. Strain the milk and gradually blend into the roux.

4 Return to the heat and bring to a boil, stirring, until the sauce thickens. Season and add any flavorings.

Salads

*Salads are such a versatile way of eating, and the variety of ingredients
is so great, that they can be made to suit any occasion, from a light piquant
starter to a more substantial dish to serve as a main course, or a mixture
of exotic fruits for a delicious dessert.*

SALAD INGREDIENTS

A salad is the ideal emergency meal. It is quick to "rustle up" and there are times when you might discover that you already have a really good combination of ingredients on hand when you need to present a meal-in-a-moment. A splash of culinary inspiration, and you will find you have prepared a fantastic salad that you had no idea was lurking in your kitchen!

Salads can be fruity, eggy, cheesy, made with grains or legumes, or just fresh green—all are highly nutritious. They are also generally low in calories if you go easy on the dressing, or use a fat-free dressing. It is easy to make a salad look attractive and appetizing, thus encouraging your family to eat fruit and vegetables. It is also often a welcome dish to serve alongside richer offerings.

Supermarkets now stock many unusual ingredients, which can add interest to an ordinary salad. Experiment with new

fruits and vegetables, buying them in small quantities to lend unusual flavors to salads made from cheaper ingredients. Always use the freshest ingredients to ensure a successful salad. Try to ensure that you buy fruit and vegetables at their peak and use them within a few days of buying.

Herbs
Every salad can be turned into something special with the addition of a few carefully chosen herbs to add flavor and a delicious aroma. The recipes in this book make liberal use of fresh herbs, adding a unique "zip" to the food. Experiment with different varieties each time you make a salad or a dressing; try marjoram, thyme, chives, basil, mint, fennel, and dill as well as the ubiquitous parsley. Basil goes especially well with tomatoes, and fennel or dill are particularly good with cucumber or beetroot salads.

Flowers
For an extra-special salad, add a few edible flowers, which look particularly colorful and attractive especially when mixed with a variety of salad greens. Common sense is the best guide as to which flowers may be used whole and which should have the petals gently separated from the calyx. Borage, primroses, violas, pot marigolds, nasturtiums, violets, rock geraniums, and rose petals are all suitable, imparting a sweetness and intense color contrast to any green salad. Chive flowers have a good strong flavor—the pretty mauve flower heads should be separated into flowerets before sprinkling over the salad.

It is, of course, important that the flowers should look fresh and clean. If they need washing, be sure to handle with great care. Gently pat dry with paper towels and then store them in a rigid plastic container in the refrigerator until required.

It goes without saying that flowers which have been sprayed with insecticide should not be used.

Nuts
In addition to color and flavor, salads need texture, which can be achieved by combining crunchy ingredients with softer fruits and vegetables. Nuts are particularly useful in this respect, contributing a pleasant crunchiness as well as

flavor. Many nuts taste even better if they are browned before use. These include almonds, hazelnuts, pine nuts, and peanuts. To brown nuts, place them on a cookie sheet and place in a hot oven for 5–10 minutes until golden brown. Pine nuts may also be browned by placing in a dry heavy-based skillet and shaking over a high heat until golden.

Arugula The young green leaves of this plant have a distinctive warm, peppery flavor and are delicious in green salads.

Chicory A slightly bitter-tasting but attractive curly-leaved salad plant. There are two varieties: the curly frisée which has a mop head of light green frilly leaves and the escarole which has broader, smoother leaves. Before they mature, both varieties have their leaves tied together to blanch the centers, which produces tender, succulent leaves.

Chinese Cabbage These are a most useful salad ingredient available in the fall and winter months. Shred them fairly finely and use them as a base, adding bean-shoots and peppery leaves such as watercress or dandelion.

Corn Salad This is also called lamb's lettuce because its dark green leaves resemble a lamb's tongue. It is also known as mâche by the French. It is well worth looking out for when it is in season both for its flavor and its appearance.

Endive This is available from fall to spring and, with its slightly bitter flavor, makes an interesting addition to winter salads. Choose firm, tightly packed cones with yellow leaf tips. Avoid any with damaged leaves or leaf tips that are turning green as they will be rather too bitter. Red endive is also available.

Iceberg Lettuce This has pale green, densely packed leaves. It may appear expensive, but is in fact extremely good value when compared with other lettuces by weight. It has a fresh, crisp texture and keeps well in the refrigerator.

Oak Leaf This red-tinged, delicately flavored lettuce is good when mixed with other leaves, both for the contrast in flavor and the contrast in color.

Purslane This has fleshy stalks and rosettes of succulent green leaves which have a sharp, clean flavor.

Radicchio This is a variety of endive originating in Italy. It looks rather like a small, tightly packed red lettuce. It is quite expensive but comparatively few leaves are needed, as it has a bitter flavor. The leaves are a deep purple color with a white contrasting rib. They add character to any green salad.

Romaine Lettuce This is a superb variety used especially in Caesar salad. It has long, narrow, bright green leaves with a wonderfully crisp texture.

Round or Cabbage Lettuce This one is the most familiar to us all. Try to avoid the hothouse variety as the leaves are limp and floppy.

Salad greens

Supermarkets now stock a wonderful variety of previously-hard-to-find salad greens, so experiment with different types. The raw leaves from young leafy vegetables can also be used.

Watercress This has a fresh peppery taste which makes it a welcome addition to many salads. It is available throughout the year, although it is less good when flowering, or early in the season when the leaves are small.

PREPARING SALAD GREENS

Whichever salad greens you choose, they should be firm and crisp with no sign of browning or wilting. They should be handled with care because salad greens bruise easily.

To prepare, pull off and discard all damaged outer leaves and wash the remaining leaves in cold, salted water to remove any insects, then dry them thoroughly. This can be done either by patting the leaves dry with paper towels, spinning them in a salad spinner, or by placing them in a clean dish cloth, gathering up the loose ends, and swinging the dish cloth around vigorously.

Dress the salad greens just before serving. If you dress it any earlier the leaves will wilt.

DRESSINGS

All salads depend on being well dressed and so it is necessary to use the best ingredients. The principal ingredients in a salad dressing are oil and vinegar, with a variety of other flavorings that can be varied to suit the particular salad.

The choice of oil is particularly important. Oils are produced from various nuts, seeds, and beans and each has its own flavor. Unrefined oils, although more expensive, are worth using for their superior taste.

Olive Oil is the best oil for most salad dressings. Choose the green-tinged, fruity oil labelled "extra virgin" or "first pressing". It has a distinctive taste and aroma.

Sesame Oil has a strong, nutty tang and is particularly good with oriental-type salads.

Sunflower and Safflower Oil are neutral-flavored oils and can be mixed with olive oil or used alone to produce a lighter dressing. Mayonnaise made with a combination of one of these oils and olive oil has a lighter consistency than one made from olive oil only.

Walnut and Hazelnut Oil have the most wonderful flavor and aroma, and are usually mixed with olive oil in a French dressing. They are well worth their higher price and are especially good with slightly bitter salad plants such as chicory, radicchio, or spinach.

A good dressing needs a touch of acidity. Good quality vinegars such as wine, cider, sherry, or herb-flavored vinegars are ideal, but malt vinegar is far too harsh and overpowers the subtle balance of the dressing. Lemon juice may be used as a dressing and is often preferable if the salad is fruit-based.

Balsamic Vinegar is dark and mellow with a sweet/sour flavor. It is expensive but you need only a few drops or at most a teaspoonful to give a wonderful taste. It is made in the area around Modena in Italy.

Cider Vinegar is reputed to contain many healthy properties and valuable nutrients. It has a light, subtle flavor redolent of the fruit from which it is made.

Flavored Vinegars can be made from cider and wine vinegar. To do this, steep your chosen ingredient in a small bottle of vinegar for anything up to two weeks. Particularly good additions are basil, tarragon, garlic, thyme, mint, or rosemary. Raspberry wine vinegar can be made by adding about twelve raspberries to a bottle of vinegar.

Sherry Vinegar has a rich mellow flavor which blends well with walnut and hazelnut oils, but is equally good by itself.

Wine Vinegar is the one most commonly used for French dressing; either red or white will do.

SALAD DRESSINGS

Make up a large bottle of your favorite dressing. Here are some recipes for you to try:

Tomato Dressing

This completely fat-free dressing is ideal if you are counting calories.

$\frac{1}{2}$ cup tomato juice
1 garlic clove, crushed
2 tbsp lemon juice
1 tbsp soy sauce
1 tsp clear honey
2 tbsp chopped chives
salt and pepper

Put all the ingredients into a screw-top jar and shake vigorously until well mixed.

Apple & Cider Vinegar Dressing

2 tbsp sunflower oil
2 tbsp concentrated apple juice
2 tbsp cider vinegar
1 tbsp Meaux mustard
1 garlic clove, crushed
salt and pepper

Put the oil, apple juice, vinegar, mustard, garlic, and salt and pepper to taste in a screw-top jar and shake vigorously until well mixed.

Sesame Dressing

A piquant dressing with a rich creamy texture.

2 tbsp sesame seed paste
2 tbsp cider vinegar
2 tbsp medium sherry
2 tbsp sesame oil
1 tbsp soy sauce
1 garlic clove, crushed

1 Put the sesame seed paste in a bowl and gradually mix in the vinegar and sherry until smooth.

2 Add the remaining ingredients and mix together thoroughly.

Green Herb Dressing

A pale green dressing with a fresh flavor, ideal with cauliflower or broccoli.

$\frac{1}{4}$ cup parsley
$\frac{1}{4}$ cup mint
$\frac{1}{4}$ cup chives
1 garlic clove, crushed
$\frac{2}{3}$ cup natural yogurt
salt and pepper

1 Remove the stalks from the parsley and mint and put the leaves in a blender or food processor with the chives, garlic, and yogurt.

2 Add seasoning to taste. Blend until smooth, then store in the refrigerator until needed.

Wok Cookery

*Wok cookery is an excellent technique for vegetarians as it enables you to
serve up delicious dishes of crisp, tasty vegetables in minutes.*

PREPARING FOOD FOR THE WOK

Ensure all ingredients are on hand before you start to cook, otherwise the first ingredients will be overcooked before the others are ready to add. Although oriental cooks use a variety of cleavers for chopping, a sharp kitchen knife will do just as well. All ingredients should be cut into uniform sizes with as many cut surfaces exposed as possible, hence the practice of cutting on the slant or diagonal, or into julienne strips or matchsticks.

Stir-frying

This is the most popular method of cooking in a wok. Once the food has been prepared and you are ready to begin, add the oil to the wok and heat it, swirling it round until it is really hot. If it is sufficiently hot the ingredients added should sizzle and begin to cook.

Most recipes begin by cooking the onions, garlic, and ginger, because they flavor the oil. The heat may need to be lowered a little at first but must be increased again as the other ingredients are added. Gas probably gives the best results because of the speed of controlling the heat, and the fact that the curved base of the wok fits so well into the hob. Electric and solid fuel hobs are more efficient if you are using a flat-bottomed wok.

Always add the ingredients in the order they are listed in the recipe. While the food is cooking, keep stirring. When you add a sauce or liquid at the end of a recipe, first push the cooked food to the side of the wok so the sauce heats as quickly as possible, then toss the food back into the sauce over a high heat so that it boils and thickens the sauce. Serve the cooked food as soon as possible.

Deep-frying

A wok is usually used for deep-frying battered egg-and-crumbed morsels of food or food encased in pastry. The best oil to use is groundnut, which has a high smoke point and mild flavor, so it will neither burn nor impart taste to the food.

If you have a round-bottomed wok, use a metal wok stand to keep it stable during cooking. It is not necessary to preheat the wok. Simply add the oil (2½ cups should be sufficient) and heat to 350°F–375°F or until a cube of bread browns in 30 seconds.

The cooking time is determined by the size of the ingredients to be cooked, and it is essential that the oil is hot enough to seal the batter or pastry as quickly as possible without the food absorbing any more oil than necessary. When golden brown, remove with a slotted spoon and drain on paper towels. Serve at once to retain the food's crispness.

Steaming

To steam food you need a large wok and a bamboo steamer with a lid. The wok needs a little water in the bottom but it must not reach the base of the bamboo steamer when it is in position: stand the steamer on a trivet. The steamer has several layers, which can be stacked on top of each other. This means more than one type of food can be cooked at the same time. Put the food on a plate that will just fit into the steamer and place it carefully in one of the layers. Add seasoning, herbs, and flavorings, cover with the lid, and steam until tender. Make sure the wok does not boil dry by adding extra water when necessary.

If you don't have a bamboo steamer, you can still steam food in the wok. Simply put a plate on a metal or wooden trivet in the wok, pour in enough water to come just below the plate, and cover with a lid.

Braising/Simmering

The wok can also be used as a saucepan and is excellent for making stir-fry soups, for example. Just stir-fry the ingredients in a little oil, add the liquid seasonings, and simmer either uncovered or with a lid. With this type of soup the vegetables should still have a good "bite" to them, so the cooking time is a lot less than that of traditional soups.

Pan-frying and braising are speeded up using a wok because of the improved heat distribution. Simply fry the ingredients quickly, then add the stock or sauce, cover, and simmer gently until tender. Sometimes it is better not to cover the wok so that the cooking liquid is reduced, intensifying the flavors even more. Whichever method is used, stir occasionally to prevent any possibility of sticking.

Vegetarian Barbecues

There are so many tasty and nutritious vegetarian dishes that can be cooked over hot coals —after all, barbecueing is just an alternative method of cooking by direct heat.

PLANNING YOUR BARBECUE

Barbecues always take longer to get going than you expect, so allow plenty of time. Don't be tempted to start cooking too soon, or the coals will not be ready. The flames should have died down and the coals reduced to a steady glow before you begin.

Don't attempt to cook for a large party on a small barbecue, as it could take hours to feed everyone! In this situation, it is better to cook most of the food in the kitchen, and either provide only a few barbecued items, or use the barbecue to finish partly-cooked foods. Vegetarian sausages and burgers are ideal, as they cook quickly and in large quantities.

ADVANCE PREPARATIONS

Many foods for barbecuing will benefit from being marinated, especially dishes using bean curd or mycoprotein, which absorb the flavor of the marinade. You can buy bean curd in four varieties—smoked, firm, soft, or silken; use smoked or firm for kabobs, soft for adding to burgers, and silken for adding to sauces and dips.

Have your kabobs ready-threaded for quick cooking; if possible, choose flat metal skewers so that the food does not slide as the kabobs are turned. Alternatively, use bamboo sticks, but soak them in water beforehand so that they do not burn over the hot coals and ruin the food.

Control the heat by adjusting the distance of the food from the coals, or by altering the controls on a gas barbecue. Ideally, food should not be cooked too quickly, or it will blacken and char on the outside before the middle is cooked—it needs time for the distinctive barbecued taste to be imparted.

COOKING TIPS

First and foremost, treat food for barbecuing with care—it should be kept chilled in the refrigerator or in a cool box, complete with ice packs, until ready to cook.

Light the barbecue in plenty of time, remembering that you will need about 45 minutes for charcoal to heat and about 10–15 minutes for a gas barbecue to become hot enough. Food cooks best over glowing embers, not smoking fuel, so avoid putting the food over the hot coals until the smoking has subsided. Oil the barbecue rack lightly before adding the food, to help to prevent it from sticking, and oil the skewers, tongs, and barbecue fork for the same reason.

Throw some fresh herbs onto the coals—they smell wonderful as they burn, and will add extra flavor to your food. Woody herbs burn slowly, so they are good choices.

COOKING VEGETABLES

For kabobs, choose a mixture of vegetables that will all cook at the same rate, and cut into even-sized chunks. Choose from eggplants, tomatoes, sliced corn-on-the-cob or baby corn cobs, mushrooms, and zucchini. New potatoes, onions, carrots, parsnips, and Jerusalem artichokes can also be barbecued, but will need pre-cooking first.

If you are going to serve jacket potatoes, cook them first too—either conventionally or in a microwave. Wrap in foil and keep warm to one side of the barbecue, ready for filling. Or finish cooking potatoes directly on the grid over the coals, barbecueing them until the skins are crisp and brown.

Vegetables can be cooked in foil packets as well as on kabob skewers. Slice them roughly, sprinkle with olive oil, herbs, and seasonings, and wrap tightly. Cook until tender.

Soups & Starters

Soup is simple to make but produces tasty results. A wide variety of soups can be made with vegetables—they can be rich and creamy, thick and chunky, light and delicate, and hot or chilled. The secret of a good soup lies in using a well-flavored stock as the base. Although there are some excellent vegetable stock cubes available, a homemade stock (see page 14) gives the edge to any soup. A wide range of ingredients can be used in addition to vegetables—try using legumes, grains, noodles, vegetarian cheese, and yogurt.

With so many fresh ingredients available, it is easy to create delicious starters that are the perfect introduction to a vegetarian meal. The ideas in this chapter are an inspiration to cook and a treat to eat, and they give an edge to the appetite that makes the main course even more enjoyable. A balance of flavors, colors, and textures will offer variety and contrast.

Red Bell Pepper & Chili Soup

This soup has a real Mediterranean flavor, using sweet red bell peppers, tomato, chili, and basil. It is great served with a warm olive bread.

Serves 4
8 ounces red bell peppers, seeded and sliced
1 onion, sliced
2 garlic cloves, crushed
1 green chili, chopped
$1^{1}/_{2}$ cups sieved tomatoes
$2^{1}/_{2}$ cups vegetable stock
2 tbsp chopped basil
fresh basil sprigs, to garnish

1 Put the bell peppers in a large saucepan with the onion, garlic, and chili. Add the sieved tomatoes and stock and bring to a boil, stirring well.

2 Reduce the heat to a simmer and cook for 20 minutes or until the bell peppers have softened. Drain, reserving the liquid and vegetables separately.

3 Sieve the vegetables by pressing through a strainer with the back of a spoon, or blend in a food processor until smooth.

4 Return the vegetable purée to a clean saucepan with the reserved cooking liquid. Add the basil and heat through until hot. Garnish and serve.

COOK'S VARIATION

This soup is also delicious served cold with $^{2}/_{3}$ cup of natural yogurt swirled into it.

Avocado & Mint Soup

A rich and creamy pale green soup made with avocados and enhanced by a touch of chopped mint. Serve chilled in summer or hot in winter.

Serves 4-6

3 tbsp butter or vegetarian margarine

6 scallions, sliced

1 garlic clove, crushed

$^1/_4$ cup all-purpose flour

$2^1/_2$ cups Fresh Vegetable Stock (see page 14)

2 ripe avocados

2–3 tsp lemon juice

good pinch of grated lemon rind

$^2/_3$ cup milk

$^2/_3$ cup light cream

1–$1^1/_2$ tbsp chopped fresh mint

salt and pepper

sprigs of fresh mint, to garnish

MINTED GARLIC BREAD

$^1/_2$ cup butter

1–2 tbsp chopped fresh mint

1–2 garlic cloves, crushed

1 whole wheat or white French bread stick

1 Melt the butter or vegetarian margarine in a large saucepan. Add the scallions and garlic and fry gently for about 3 minutes until soft but not colored.

2 Stir in the flour and cook for 1–2 minutes. Gradually stir in the stock then bring to a boil. Let simmer gently while preparing the avocados.

3 Peel the avocados, discard the pits, and chop the flesh. Add to the soup with the lemon juice and rind and salt and pepper to taste. Cover and simmer for about 10 minutes or until tender.

4 Cool the soup slightly then press through a strainer or blend in a food processor or blender until smooth. Pour into a bowl.

5 Stir in the milk and cream, adjust the seasoning, then stir in the mint. Cover and chill thoroughly.

6 To make the garlic bread, soften the butter and beat in the mint and garlic.

Cut the loaf into slanting slices, but do not cut all the way through—leave the slices attached at the base. Spread each slice with the garlic butter and reassemble the loaf. Wrap in foil and place in a preheated oven at 350°F for 15 minutes.

7 Serve the soup garnished with a sprig of mint and accompanied by the minted garlic bread.

Mixed Bean Soup

This is a really hearty soup, filled with color, flavor, and goodness,
which may be adapted to any vegetables that you have to hand.

Serves 4
1 tbsp vegetable oil
1 red onion, halved and sliced
3$^{1}/_{2}$ ounces potato, diced
1 carrot, diced
1 leek, sliced
1 green chili, sliced
3 garlic cloves, crushed
1 tsp ground coriander
1 tsp chili powder
4 cups vegetable stock
1 pound mixed canned beans, such as red kidney, borlotti, black eye, or flageolet, drained
salt and pepper
2 tbsp chopped cilantro, to garnish

1 Heat the oil in a large saucepan and add the onion, potato, carrot, and leek. Sauté for 2 minutes, stirring, until slightly softened. Add the chili and garlic and cook for another minute.

2 Stir in the ground coriander, chili powder and the stock. Bring to a boil, reduce the heat, and cook for 20 minutes or until the vegetables are tender.

3 Stir in the beans, season to taste, and cook for a further 10 minutes. Garnish with chopped cilantro and serve.

COOK'S TIP

Serve this soup with slices of warm corn bread or a cheese loaf.

Noodle, Mushroom, & Ginger Soup

Thai soups are very quickly and easily put together, and are cooked
so that each ingredient can still be tasted in the finished dish.

Serves 4
$^{1}/_{2}$ ounce dried Chinese mushrooms or $4^{1}/_{2}$ ounces field or crimini mushrooms
4 cups hot Fresh Vegetable Stock (see page 14)
$4^{1}/_{2}$ ounces thread egg noodles
2 tsp sunflower oil
3 garlic cloves, crushed
1 inch piece ginger shredded finely
$^{1}/_{2}$ tsp mushroom ketchup
1 tsp light soy sauce
2 cups bean sprouts
fresh cilantro leaves, to garnish

1 Soak the dried Chinese
mushrooms, if using, in 1¼ cups of
the hot vegetable stock for at least
30 minutes. Remove the stalks and
discard, then slice the mushrooms.
Reserve the stock.

2 Cook the noodles in a saucepan of
boiling water for 2–3 minutes. Drain,
rinse, and drain again. Set aside
until required.

3 Heat the oil over a high heat in a
wok or large, heavy skillet. Add the
garlic and ginger, stirring. Add the
mushrooms and cook over a high heat
for 2 minutes, stirring well.

4 Add the remaining vegetable stock,
with the reserved hot stock and bring
to a boil. Add the mushroom ketchup
and soy sauce.

5 Stir in the bean sprouts and cook
until tender.

6 Pour the soup over the noodles,
garnish, and serve.

COOK'S TIP

Dried Chinese mushrooms are
available from oriental stores.

Jerusalem Artichoke Soup

Jerusalem artichokes belong to the tuber family. They are native
to North America, but are also grown in Europe. They have a delicious nutty flavor
which combines well with the orange in this soup.

Serves 4
1¹/₂ pounds Jerusalem artichokes
5 tbsp orange juice
2 tbsp butter
1 leek, chopped
1 garlic clove, crushed
1¹/₄ cups vegetable stock
²/₃ cup milk
2 tbsp chopped cilantro
²/₃ cup natural yogurt
grated orange rind, to garnish

1 Rinse the Jerusalem artichokes
and place in a large saucepan with
2 tablespoons of the orange juice and
enough water to cover. Bring to a
boil, reduce the heat and cook for
20 minutes or until the artichokes are
tender. Drain the artichokes, reserving
2 cups of the cooking liquid. Leave
the artichokes to cool.

2 Peel the artichokes and mash the
flesh with a potato masher.

3 Melt the butter in a large saucepan
and sauté the leek and garlic for
2–3 minutes, stirring until the leek
softens.

4 Stir in the artichoke flesh, the
reserved cooking water, the stock,
milk, and remaining orange juice.
Bring the soup to a boil, reduce the
heat, and simmer for 2–3 minutes.

5 Reserving a few pieces of leek,
transfer the remainder of the soup
to a food processor and blend for
1 minute until smooth.

6 Return the soup to a clean saucepan
and stir in the reserved leeks, cilantro,
and yogurt.

7 Transfer to individual soup bowls,
garnish with orange rind, and serve.

COOK'S VARIATION

If Jerusalem artichokes are
unavailable, you could use
sweet potatoes instead.

Fava Bean & Mint Soup

Fresh fava beans are best for this recipe, but if they are unavailable, use frozen beans instead. They combine well with the fresh flavor of mint.

Serves 4
2 tbsp olive oil
1 red onion, chopped
2 garlic cloves, crushed
2 potatoes, diced
1 pound fava beans, thawed if frozen
$3^3/_4$ cups vegetable stock
2 tbsp freshly chopped mint
fresh mint sprigs and yogurt, to garnish

1 Heat the oil in a large saucepan and sauté the onion and garlic for 2–3 minutes until softened.

2 Add the potatoes and cook for 5 minutes, stirring well. Stir in the beans and the stock, cover, and simmer for 30 minutes or until the beans and potatoes are tender.

3 Reserving a few vegetables, place the remainder of the soup in a food processor or blender and purée until smooth.

4 Return the soup to a clean saucepan and add the reserved vegetables and mint. Serve garnished with swirls of yogurt and sprigs of fresh mint.

COOK'S VARIATION

Use fresh cilantro and $1/_2$ tsp ground cumin as flavorings in the soup, if you prefer.

Garbanzo Bean & Tomato Soup

A thick vegetable soup which is a delicious meal in itself.
Serve the soup with thin shavings of Parmesan and warm ciabatta bread.

Serves 4
2 tbsp olive oil
2 leeks, sliced thinly
2 zucchini, chopped
2 garlic cloves, crushed
2 × 14 ounce cans chopped tomatoes
1 tbsp tomato paste
1 bay leaf
3¾ cups Fresh Vegetable Stock (see page 14)
14 ounce can garbanzo beans, drained
8 ounces spinach
salt and pepper
thin shavings of Parmesan, to garnish (optional)
crusty bread, to serve

1 Heat the oil in a saucepan, add the leeks and zucchini, and cook briskly for 5 minutes, stirring constantly.

2 Add the garlic, tomatoes, tomato paste, bay leaf, stock, and garbanzo beans. Bring to a boil and simmer for 5 minutes.

3 Shred the spinach finely, add to the soup, and boil for 2 minutes. Season with salt and pepper to taste.

4 Remove the bay leaf from the soup and discard.

5 Pour the soup into a soup tureen or into individual soup bowls and sprinkle with shavings of Parmesan, if using. Serve with crusty bread.

Vegetable & Corn Chowder

This is a really filling soup, which should be served before a lighter meal.
Packed with corn and fresh vegetables it is easy to prepare and filled with flavor.

Serves 4
1 tbsp vegetable oil
1 red onion, diced
1 red bell pepper, diced
3 garlic cloves, crushed
1 large potato, diced
2 tbsp all-purpose flour
2¹/₂ cups milk
1¹/₄ cups vegetable stock
1³/₄ ounces broccoli florets
3 cups canned corn
in brine, drained
³/₄ cup vegetarian
Cheddar cheese, grated
salt and pepper
1 tbsp chopped fresh cilantro, to garnish

COOK'S TIP

Vegetarian cheeses are made with rennets of non-animal origin, using microbial or fungal enzymes.

COOK'S TIP

Add a little heavy cream to the soup after adding the milk for a really creamy flavor.

1 Heat the oil in a large saucepan and sauté the onion, bell peppers, garlic, and potato for 2–3 minutes, stirring.

2 Stir in the flour and cook for 30 seconds. Stir in the milk and stock.

3 Add the broccoli and corn. Bring the mixture to a boil, stirring, then reduce the heat, and simmer for about 20 minutes or until the vegetables are tender.

4 Stir in ¹/₂ cup of the cheese until it melts.

5 Season and spoon the chowder into a warm soup tureen. Garnish with the remaining cheese and the cilantro and serve immediately.

Gardener's Broth

This thick, hearty soup uses a variety of green vegetables with a flavoring of ground coriander. A finishing touch of thinly sliced leeks adds texture.

Serves 4
3 tbsp butter or vegetarian margarine
1 onion, chopped
1–2 garlic cloves, crushed
1 large leek
8 ounces Brussels sprouts
4^1/$_2$ ounces green or runner beans
5 cups Fresh Vegetable Stock (see page 14)
4^1/$_2$ ounces frozen peas
1 tbsp lemon juice
^{1}/$_2$ tsp ground coriander
4 tbsp heavy cream
salt and pepper
MELBA TOAST
4–6 slices white bread

1 Melt the butter or vegetarian margarine in a saucepan, add the onion and garlic, and fry very gently, stirring occasionally, until they begin to soften but not color.

2 Using a sharp knife, slice the white part of the leek very thinly and reserve; slice the green parts of the leek. Slice the Brussels sprouts and thinly slice the beans.

3 Add the green part of the leeks, the Brussels sprouts, and beans to the saucepan. Add the stock and bring to a boil. Simmer for 10 minutes.

4 Add the frozen peas, seasoning, lemon juice, and ground coriander and simmer for 10–15 minutes or until the vegetables are tender.

5 Cool the soup a little, then press through a strainer or blend in a food processor or blender until smooth. Pour into a clean pan.

6 Add the reserved slices of leek to the soup, bring back to a boil, and simmer for about 5 minutes until the leeks are tender. Adjust the seasoning

according to taste, stir in the cream, and reheat gently.

7 To make the melba toast, toast the bread on both sides under a preheated broiler. Cut horizontally through the slices then toast the uncooked sides until they curl up. Serve immediately with the soup.

Gazpacho

This Spanish soup is full of chopped and grated vegetables with a puréed tomato base.
Serve with extra chopped vegetables and croutons.

Serves 4
½ small cucumber
½ small green bell pepper, chopped very finely
1 pound 2 ounces ripe tomatoes, peeled or 14 ounce can chopped tomatoes
½ onion, chopped coarsely
2–3 garlic cloves, crushed
3 tbsp olive oil
2 tbsp white wine vinegar
1–2 tbsp lemon or lime juice
2 tbsp tomato paste
scant 2 cups tomato juice
salt and pepper
TO SERVE
chopped green bell pepper
thinly sliced onion rings
garlic croutons

1 Coarsely grate the cucumber into a bowl and add the chopped green bell pepper, mixing well.

2 Blend the tomatoes, onion, and garlic in a food processor or blender, then add the oil, vinegar, lemon or lime juice, and tomato paste and blend until smooth. Alternatively, finely chop the tomatoes and finely grate the onion, then mix both with the garlic, oil, vinegar, lemon or lime juice, and tomato paste.

3 Add the tomato mixture to the cucumber and green bell pepper mixture and combine.

4 Add the tomato juice and mix again.

5 Season with salt and pepper to taste, cover the bowl with plastic wrap, and chill thoroughly for at least 6 hours, but preferably longer for the flavors to combine.

6 Prepare the side dishes of green bell pepper, onion rings, and garlic croutons to serve and arrange in individual serving bowls.

7 Ladle the soup into bowls, preferably from a soup tureen set on the table with the side dishes around it. Hand the dishes around to allow the guests to help themselves.

Cauliflower & Broccoli Soup with Gruyère

Full of flavor, this creamy cauliflower and broccoli soup is simple to make and delicious to eat.

Serves 4
3 tbsp vegetable oil
1 red onion, chopped
2 garlic cloves, crushed
$10\frac{1}{2}$ ounces cauliflower florets
$10\frac{1}{2}$ ounces broccoli florets
1 tbsp all-purpose flour
$2\frac{1}{2}$ cups milk
$1\frac{1}{4}$ cups vegetable stock
$\frac{3}{4}$ cup vegetarian Gruyère cheese, grated
pinch of paprika
$\frac{2}{3}$ cup light cream
paprika and vegetarian Gruyère cheese shavings, to garnish

1 Heat the oil in a large saucepan and sauté the onion, garlic, cauliflower, and broccoli for 3–4 minutes, stirring constantly.

2 Add the flour and cook for a further 1 minute, stirring.

3 Stir in the milk and stock and bring to a boil. Reduce the heat and simmer for 20 minutes or until the vegetables are tender.

4 Remove about a quarter of the vegetable pieces with a slotted spoon, set aside, and reserve until required.

5 Put the remaining soup in a food processor and blend for 30 seconds until smooth. Transfer the soup to a clean saucepan.

6 Return the reserved vegetable pieces to the soup.

7 Stir in the cheese, paprika, and cream and heat gently for 2–3 minutes without boiling, or until the cheese starts to melt.

8 Transfer to warm serving bowls, garnish with shavings of Gruyère, and dust with paprika.

COOK'S TIP

The soup must not start to boil after the cream has been added otherwise it will curdle. Use natural yogurt instead of the cream if preferred, but again do not allow to boil.

Beetroot Soup

Here are two variations using the same vegetable: a creamy soup made
with puréed cooked beetroot; and a traditional clear soup, Borscht.

Serves 4–6
BORSCHT
1 pound 2 ounces raw beetroot, peeled and grated
2 carrots, chopped finely
1 large onion, chopped finely
1 garlic clove, crushed
1 bouquet garni
5 cups Fresh Vegetable Stock (see page 14)
2–3 tsp lemon juice
salt and pepper
$^2/_3$ cup sour cream, to serve
CREAMED BEETROOT SOUP
$^1/_4$ cup butter or vegetarian margarine
2 large onions, chopped finely
1–2 carrots, chopped
2 celery sticks, chopped
1 pound 2 ounces cooked beetroot, diced
1–2 tbsp lemon juice
$3^1/_2$ cups Fresh Vegetable Stock (see page 14)
$1^1/_4$ cups milk
salt and pepper
TO SERVE
grated cooked beetroot or 6 tbsp sour or heavy cream, lightly whipped

1 To make borscht, place the beetroot, carrots, onion, garlic, bouquet garni, stock, lemon juice, and seasoning in a large saucepan. Bring to a boil, cover, and simmer for 45 minutes, stirring occasionally.

2 Press the soup through a fine strainer or a strainer lined with cheesecloth, then pour into a clean pan. Adjust the seasoning and add extra lemon juice if necessary. Bring to a boil and simmer for 1–2 minutes. Serve with a spoonful of sour cream swirled through.

3 To make creamed beetroot soup, melt the butter or margarine in a pan and fry the onions, carrots, and celery until just beginning to color.

4 Add the beetroot, 1 tablespoon of lemon juice, the stock, and seasoning and bring to a boil. Cover and simmer for 30 minutes until tender.

5 Cool slightly, then press through a strainer or blend in a food processor or blender. Pour into a clean pan, add the milk, and bring to a boil. Adjust the seasoning and add extra lemon juice if necessary. Serve.

Dahl Soup

Dahl is a name given to a delicious Indian lentil dish.
This soup is a variation of the theme—it is made with red lentils
and spiced with curry powder.

Serves 4
2 tbsp butter
2 garlic cloves, crushed
1 onion, chopped
$1/2$ tsp turmeric
1 tsp garam masala
$1/4$ tsp chili powder
1 tsp ground cumin
2 pounds 4 ounces canned, chopped tomatoes, drained
1 cup red lentils
2 tsp lemon juice
$2^1/2$ cups vegetable stock
$1^1/4$ cups coconut milk
chopped cilantro and lemon slices, to garnish
nan bread, to serve

1 Melt the butter in a large saucepan and sauté the garlic and onion for 2–3 minutes, stirring. Add the spices and cook for a further 30 seconds.

2 Stir in the tomatoes, lentils, lemon juice, stock, and coconut milk and bring to a boil. Reduce the heat and simmer for 25–30 minutes until the lentils are tender and cooked.

3 Season and spoon the soup into a warm tureen. Garnish and serve with warm nan bread.

COOK'S TIP

Add small quantities of hot water to the pan whilst the lentils are cooking if they begin to absorb too much of the liquid.

Vichyssoise

This is a classic creamy soup made from potatoes and leeks.
To achieve the delicate pale color, be sure to use only the white parts of the leeks.

Serves 4–6
3 large leeks
3 tbsp butter
or vegetarian margarine
1 onion, sliced thinly
1 pound 2 ounces potatoes, chopped
3¹/₂ cups Fresh Vegetable Stock
(see page 14)
2 tsp lemon juice
pinch of ground nutmeg
¹/₄ tsp ground coriander
1 bay leaf
1 egg yolk
²/₃ cup light cream
salt and white pepper
snipped chives, to garnish

1 Trim the leeks and remove most of the green part—it can be served as a vegetable. Slice the white part of the leeks very finely.

2 Melt the butter or margarine in a saucepan and gently fry the leeks and onion, stirring from time to time, for about 5 minutes until they are soft but not brown.

3 Add the potatoes, stock, lemon juice, salt and white pepper to taste, ground nutmeg, ground coriander, and bay leaf to the pan and bring to a boil. Cover and simmer for about 30 minutes or until all of the vegetables are very soft.

4 Leave the soup to cool a little then discard the bay leaf. Press the soup through a strainer or blend in a food processor or blender until smooth. Pour the soup into a clean saucepan.

5 Blend the egg yolk into the cream. Add a little of the soup to the egg and cream mixture and then whisk it all back into the soup and reheat gently without boiling. Add a little more salt and white pepper to taste, if necessary. Cool and chill thoroughly before serving.

6 Serve the soup sprinkled with freshly snipped chives.

Curried Parsnip Soup

Parsnips make a delicious soup as they have a slightly sweet flavor. In this recipe, spices are added to complement this sweetness and a dash of lemon juice adds tartness.

Serves 4
1 tbsp vegetable oil
1 tbsp butter
1 red onion, chopped
3 parsnips, chopped
2 garlic cloves, crushed
2 tsp garam masala
1/2 tsp chili powder
1 tbsp all-purpose flour
3 3/4 cups vegetable stock
grated rind and juice of 1 lemon
salt and pepper
lemon zest, to garnish

1 Heat the oil and butter in a large saucepan until the butter has melted.

2 Add the onion, parsnips, and garlic and sauté for 5–7 minutes, stirring, until the vegetables have softened.

3 Add the garam masala and chili powder and cook for 30 seconds, stirring well.

4 Sprinkle in the flour, mixing well, and cook for a further 30 seconds.

5 Stir in the stock, lemon rind, and juice, and bring to a boil. Reduce the heat and simmer for 20 minutes or until the parsnips are tender.

6 Remove some of the vegetable pieces with a slotted spoon and reserve until required. Blend the remaining soup and vegetables in a food processor for 1 minute or until smooth.

7 Return the soup to a clean saucepan and stir in the reserved vegetables. Heat the soup through for 2 minutes.

8 Transfer to soup bowls, garnish with grated lemon zest, and serve.

COOK'S VARIATION

Use 1 medium orange instead of the lemon, if preferred, and garnish with grated orange zest.

Avocado & Vegetable Soup

Avocado has a rich flavor and color which makes a creamy flavored soup.
It is best served chilled, but may be eaten warm as well.

Serves 4
1 large, ripe avocado
2 tbsp lemon juice
1 tbsp vegetable oil
$^{1}/_{2}$ cup canned corn, drained
2 tomatoes, peeled and seeded
1 garlic clove, crushed
1 leek, chopped
1 red chili, chopped
2 cups vegetable stock
$^{2}/_{3}$ cup milk
shredded leeks, to garnish

1 Peel and mash the avocado with a fork, stir in the lemon juice, and reserve until required.

2 Heat the oil in a pan and sauté the corn, tomatoes, garlic, leek, and chili for 2–3 minutes until softened.

3 Put half of the vegetable mixture in a food processor or blender with the avocado and blend until smooth. Transfer to a clean saucepan.

4 Add the stock and milk and reserved vegetables and cook gently for 3–4 minutes until hot. Garnish with shredded leeks and serve.

COOK'S TIP

If serving chilled, transfer from the food processor to a bowl, stir in the stock and milk, cover, and chill in the refrigerator for at least 4 hours.

Soft Cheese & Fresh Herb Soup

Make the most of home-grown herbs to create this wonderfully
creamy soup with its marvellous garden-fresh fragrance.

Serves 4
2 tbsp butter or vegetarian margarine
2 onions, chopped
3¹/₂ cups Fresh Vegetable Stock (see page 14)
2 tbsp coarsely chopped mixed fresh herbs, such as parsley, chives, thyme, basil, and oregano
1 cup full-fat soft cheese
1 tbsp cornstarch
1 tbsp milk
snipped fresh chives, to garnish

1 Melt the butter or margarine in a large saucepan and add the onions. Fry for 2 minutes, then cover, and reduce the heat to low. Allow the onions to cook gently for 5 minutes, then remove the lid.

2 Add the stock and herbs to the saucepan. Bring to a boil, then reduce the heat. Cover and simmer gently for 20 minutes.

3 Remove the saucepan from the heat. Blend the soup in a food processor or blender for about 15 seconds, until smooth. Alternatively, press it through a strainer using the back of a spoon. Return the soup to the saucepan.

4 Spoon the soft cheese into the soup and whisk until fully incorporated.

5 Mix the cornstarch with the milk, then stir into the soup and heat,

stirring constantly, until thickened and smooth. Pour the soup into 4 warmed bowls. Garnish with snipped chives and serve at once.

COOK'S TIP

Cheese is a good source of vitamins.

Celery, Stilton, & Walnut Soup

This is a classic combination of ingredients all brought
together in a delicious, creamy soup.

Serves 4
4 tbsp butter
2 shallots, chopped
3 celery sticks, chopped
1 garlic clove, crushed
2 tbsp all-purpose flour
2½ cups vegetable stock
1¼ cups milk
1½ cups blue Stilton cheese crumbled, plus extra to garnish
2 tbsp walnut halves, roughly chopped
⅔ cup natural yogurt
salt and pepper
chopped celery leaves, to garnish

1 Melt the butter in a large saucepan and sauté the shallots, celery, and garlic for 2–3 minutes, stirring, until softened.

2 Add the flour and cook for 30 seconds.

3 Gradually stir in the stock and milk and bring to a boil.

4 Reduce the heat to a gentle simmer and add the cheese and walnuts. Cover and leave to simmer for 20 minutes.

5 Stir in the yogurt and heat for a further 2 minutes without boiling.

6 Transfer to a warm soup tureen or individual serving bowls, garnish with chopped celery leaves and extra crumbled blue Stilton cheese and serve at once.

COOK'S TIP

As well as adding protein, vitamins, and useful fats to the diet, nuts add important flavor and texture to vegetarian meals.

COOK'S VARIATION

Use an alternative blue cheese, such as Dolcelatte or Gorgonzola, if preferred, or a strong vegetarian Cheddar cheese, grated.

Pumpkin Soup

This is an American classic that has now become popular worldwide.
When pumpkin is out of season use butternut squash instead.

Serves 4–6
2 pounds 4 ounces pumpkin
3 tbsp butter or vegetarian margarine
1 onion, sliced thinly
1 garlic clove, crushed
3¹/₂ cups Fresh Vegetable Stock (see page 14)
¹/₂ tsp ground ginger
1 tbsp lemon juice
3–4 thinly pared strips of orange rind (optional)
1–2 bay leaves or 1 bouquet garni
1¹/₄ cups milk
salt and pepper

TO GARNISH

4–6 tablespoons light or heavy cream, natural yogurt, or fromage frais
snipped fresh chives

1 Peel the pumpkin, remove the seeds, and then cut the flesh into 1 inch cubes.

2 Melt the butter or margarine in a large saucepan, add the onion and garlic, and fry gently until soft but not colored.

3 Add the pumpkin and toss with the onion for 1–2 minutes.

4 Add the stock and bring to a boil. Add the ginger, lemon juice, strips of orange rind, if using, bay leaves or bouquet garni, and salt and pepper to taste. Cover and simmer gently for about 20 minutes or until the pumpkin is very tender.

5 Discard the orange rind, if using, and the bay leaves or bouquet garni. Cool the soup a little and then press through a strainer, or blend in a food processor or blender until smooth. Pour the soup into a clean saucepan.

6 Add the milk and reheat gently. Adjust the seasoning to taste. Garnish with a swirl of cream, natural yogurt, or fromage frais and snipped chives Serve immediately.

Hot & Sour Soup

A very traditional staple of the Thai national diet, this soup is sold on street corners, at food bars, and by mobile vendors all over the country.

Serves 4
1 tbsp sunflower oil
8 ounces smoked bean curd, sliced
3 ounces shiitake mushrooms, sliced
2 tbsp chopped fresh cilantro
4½ ounces watercress
1 red chili, sliced finely, to garnish

STOCK
1 tbsp tamarind pulp
2 dried red chilies, chopped
2 kaffir lime leaves, torn in half
1 inch piece ginger root, chopped
2 inch piece galangal, chopped
1 stalk lemon grass, chopped
1 onion, quartered
4 cups cold water

1 Put all the ingredients for the stock into a saucepan and bring to a boil. Simmer for 5 minutes. Remove from the heat and strain, reserving the stock.

2 Heat the oil in a wok or large, heavy skillet and cook the bean curd over a high heat for about 2 minutes, stirring constantly. Pour in the strained stock.

3 Add the mushrooms and cilantro and boil for 3 minutes. Add the watercress and boil for 1 minute. Serve at once, garnished with chili slices, if wished.

Spanish Tomato Soup

This Mediterranean tomato soup is thickened with bread,
as is traditional in some parts of Spain.

Serves 4
4 tbsp olive oil
1 onion, chopped
3 garlic cloves, crushed
1 green bell pepper, chopped
$\frac{1}{2}$ tsp chili powder
1 pound tomatoes, chopped
8 ounces French or Italian bread, cubed
4 cups vegetable stock

GARLIC BREAD
4 slices ciabatta or French bread
4 tbsp olive oil
2 garlic cloves, crushed
$\frac{1}{4}$ cup grated vegetarian Cheddar
chili powder, to garnish

1 Heat the oil in a large skillet and sauté the onion, garlic, and bell pepper for 2–3 minutes, or until the onion has softened.

2 Add the chili powder and tomatoes and cook over a medium heat until the mixture has thickened.

3 Stir in the bread and stock and cook for 10–15 minutes until the soup is thick and fairly smooth.

4 To make the garlic bread, toast the bread slices under a medium broiler. Drizzle the oil over the top of the bread, rub with the garlic, sprinkle with the cheese, and return to the broiler for 2–3 minutes until the cheese has melted. Sprinkle with chili powder and serve with the soup.

Mixed Bahjis

These small bahjis are served in Indian restaurants as accompaniments to a main meal, but they are delicious as a starter with a small salad and yogurt sauce.

Serves 4
BAHJIS
1¼ cups gram flour
1 tsp bicarbonate of soda
2 tsp ground coriander
1 tsp garam masala
1½ tsp turmeric
1½ tsp chili powder
2 tbsp chopped cilantro
1 small onion, halved and sliced
1 small leek, sliced
3½ ounces cooked cauliflower
9-12 tbsp cold water
salt and pepper
vegetable oil, for deep-frying
SAUCE
²/₃ cup natural yogurt
2 tbsp chopped mint
½ tsp turmeric
1 garlic clove, crushed
fresh mint sprigs, to garnish

1 Sieve the flour, bicarbonate of soda, and salt to taste into a mixing bowl and add the spices and fresh cilantro. Mix well.

2 Divide the mixture into 3 and place in separate bowls. Stir the onion into one bowl, the leek into another, and the cauliflower into the third bowl. Add 3–4 tbsp of water to each bowl and mix each to form a smooth paste.

3 Heat the oil for deep-frying in a deep fat fryer to 350°F or until a cube of bread browns in 30 seconds. Using 2 dessert spoons, form the mixture into rounds and cook each in the oil

for 3–4 minutes until browned. Remove with a slotted spoon and drain on absorbent paper towels. Keep the bahjis warm in the oven whilst cooking the remainder.

4 Mix all of the sauce ingredients together, garnish with mint sprigs, and serve with the warm bahjis.

COOK'S VARIATION

If you prefer, use cooked broccoli instead of the cauliflower or cooked, drained spinach instead of the leek for a range of different flavored bahjis.

Fiery Salsa with Tortilla Chips

Make this Mexican-style salsa to perk up jaded palates.
Its lively flavors really get the tastebuds going.

Serves 6
2 small red chilies
1 tbsp lime or lemon juice
2 large ripe avocados
2 inch piece cucumber
2 tomatoes, peeled
1 small garlic clove, crushed
few drops of Tabasco sauce
salt and pepper
lime or lemon slices, to garnish
tortilla chips, to serve

1 Remove and discard the stem and seeds from 1 chili. Chop very finely and place in a mixing bowl. To make a chili "flower" for garnishing, slice the remaining chili from the stem to the tip several times without removing the stem. Place in a bowl of cold water, so that the "petals" open out.

2 Add the lime or lemon juice to the mixing bowl. Halve, pit, and peel the avocados. Add to the mixing bowl and mash with a fork. (The lime or lemon juice prevents the avocado from turning brown).

3 Chop the cucumber and tomatoes finely and add to the avocado mixture with the crushed garlic.

4 Season the dip to taste with Tabasco sauce, salt, and pepper.

5 Transfer the dip to a serving bowl. Garnish with slices of lime or lemon and the chili flower. Put the bowl on a large plate, surround with tortilla chips, and serve.

Hummus & Garlic Toasts

Hummus is a real favorite spread on these garlic toasts for a delicious starter or as part of a light lunch.

Serves 4
HUMMUS
14 ounce can garbanzo beans
juice of 1 large lemon
6 tbsp sesame seed paste
2 tbsp olive oil
2 garlic cloves, crushed
salt and pepper
chopped fresh cilantro
and black olives,
to garnish
TOASTS
1 ciabatta loaf, sliced
2 garlic cloves, crushed
1 tbsp chopped fresh cilantro
4 tbsp olive oil

4 Mix the garlic, cilantro, and olive oil together and drizzle over the bread slices. Cook under a hot broiler for about 2–3 minutes until golden brown, turning once. Serve hot with the hummus.

COOK'S TIP

Make the hummus 1 day in advance, and chill, covered, in the refrigerator until required. Garnish and serve.

1 To make the hummus, firstly drain the garbanzo beans, reserving a little of the liquid. Put the garbanzo beans and liquid in a food processor and blend, gradually adding the reserved liquid and lemon juice. Blend well after each addition until smooth.

2 Stir in the sesame seed paste and all but 1 teaspoon of the olive oil. Add the garlic, season with salt and pepper to taste, and blend again until smooth. Spoon the hummus into a serving dish. Drizzle the remaining olive oil over the top and garnish with chopped cilantro and olives. Leave to chill in the refrigerator while preparing the toasts.

3 Lay the slices of ciabatta on a broiler rack in a single layer.

Eggplant Dipping Platter

Dipping platters are a very sociable dish, bringing together all the diners at the table.
This substantial dip is served with vegetables as an appetizer.

Serves 4

1 eggplant, peeled
and cut into 1 inch cubes

3 tbsp sesame seeds, roasted
in a dry pan over a low heat

1 tsp sesame oil

grated rind and juice of $\frac{1}{2}$ lime

1 small shallot, diced

$\frac{1}{2}$ tsp salt

1 tsp sugar

1 red chili, deseeded and sliced

$4\frac{1}{2}$ ounces broccoli florets

2 carrots, cut into matchsticks

8 baby corn cobs,
cut in half lengthwise

2 celery stalks, cut into
matchsticks

1 baby red cabbage, cut into
8 wedges, the leaves of each wedge
held together by the core

1 Cook the diced eggplant in a saucepan of boiling water for 7–8 minutes.

2 Meanwhile, grind the sesame seeds with the oil in a food processor or pestle and mortar.

3 Add the eggplant, lime rind and juice, shallot, salt, sugar, and chili in that order to the sesame seeds. Process, or chop and mash by hand, until smooth.

4 Adjust the seasoning if necessary then spoon into a bowl. Serve the dip surrounded by the broccoli, carrots, baby corn cobs, celery, and red cabbage.

Vegetable Fritters with Sweet & Sour Sauce

These mixed vegetable fritters are coated in a light batter and deep fried until golden for a deliciously crisp coating. They are ideal with the sweet and sour dipping sauce.

Serves 4

³/₄ cup whole wheat flour

pinch of salt

pinch of cayenne pepper

4 tsp olive oil

12 tbsp cold water

3¹/₂ ounces broccoli florets

3¹/₂ ounces cauliflower florets

1³/₄ ounces snow peas

1 large carrot, cut into batons

1 red bell pepper, sliced

2 egg whites, beaten

oil, for deep-frying

SAUCE

²/₃ cup pineapple juice

²/₃ cup vegetable stock

2 tbsp wine vinegar

2 tbsp light brown sugar

2 tsp cornstarch

2 scallions, chopped

1 Sieve the flour and salt into a mixing bowl and add the cayenne pepper. Make a well in the center and gradually beat in the oil and cold water to make a smooth batter.

2 Cook the vegetables in boiling water for 5 minutes and drain well.

3 Whisk the egg whites until they form peaks and fold them into the flour batter.

4 Dip the vegetables into the batter, turning to coat well. Drain off any excess batter. Heat the oil for deep-frying in a deep fat fryer to 350°F or until a cube of bread browns in

30 seconds. Fry the vegetables for 1–2 minutes, in batches, until golden. Remove from the oil with a slotted spoon and drain on paper towels.

5 Place all of the sauce ingredients in a pan and bring to a boil, stirring, until thickened and clear. Serve with the vegetable fritters.

COOK'S VARIATION

Use any variety of vegetables that you have to hand for the fritters, such as cubes of potato or sweet potato, or green beans.

Cheese, Garlic, & Herb Pâté

This wonderful soft cheese pâté is fragrant with the aroma of fresh herbs and garlic.
Serve with triangles of Melba toast to make the perfect starter.

Serves 4
1 tbsp butter
1 garlic clove, crushed
3 scallions, chopped finely
$^{1}/_{2}$ cup full-fat soft cheese
2 tbsp chopped mixed fresh herbs, such as parsley, chives, marjoram, oregano, and basil
6 ounces sharp Cheddar
4–6 slices of white bread from a medium-cut sliced loaf
pepper
mixed salad greens and cherry tomatoes, to serve
TO GARNISH
ground paprika
sprigs of fresh herbs

1 Melt the butter in a small skillet and gently fry the garlic and scallions together for 3–4 minutes, until softened. Allow to cool.

2 Beat the soft cheese in a bowl, then add the garlic and scallions. Stir in the herbs and season with pepper to taste, mixing well.

3 Grate the Cheddar and stir into the mixture to form a stiff paste. Cover and chill in the refrigerator until ready to serve.

4 To make the Melba toast, toast the slices of bread on both sides, and then cut off the crusts.

5 Using a sharp bread knife, cut through the slices horizontally to make very thin slices.

6 Cut into triangles and then lightly broil the untoasted sides.

7 Arrange the mixed salad leaves on 4 serving plates with the cherry tomatoes. Pile the cheese pâté on top and sprinkle with a little paprika. Garnish with sprigs of fresh herbs and serve with the Melba toast.

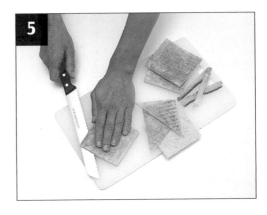

Tomato, Olive, & Mozzarella Bruschetta

These simple toasts are filled with color and flavor. They are great as a speedy starter or delicious as an appetizer with a good red wine.

Serves 4
4 muffins
4 garlic cloves, crushed
2 tbsp butter
1 tbsp chopped basil
4 large, ripe tomatoes
1 tbsp tomato paste
8 pitted black olives, halved
salt and pepper
1³/₄ ounces Mozzarella cheese, sliced
fresh basil leaves, to garnish

DRESSING
1 tbsp olive oil
2 tsp lemon juice
1 tsp clear honey

5 Return the muffins to the broiler for another 1–2 minutes until the cheese melts.

6 Garnish with fresh basil leaves and serve at once.

COOK'S VARIATION

Use balsamic vinegar instead of the lemon juice for an authentic Mediterranean flavor.

1 Cut the muffins in half to give eight thick pieces. Toast the muffin halves under a hot broiler for 2–3 minutes until golden.

2 Mix the garlic, butter, and basil together and spread on to each muffin half.

3 Cut a cross shape at the base of each tomato. Plunge the tomatoes in a bowl of boiling water—this will make the skin easier to peel. After a few minutes, pick each tomato up with a fork and peel away the skin. Chop the tomato flesh and mix with the tomato paste and olives. Divide the mixture between the muffins.

4 Mix the dressing ingredients and drizzle over each muffin. Arrange the Mozzarella cheese on top and season.

Mint & Cannellini Bean Dip

This dip is ideal for pre-dinner drinks or for handing around at a party,
accompanied by chips and colorful vegetable crudités.

Serves 6

1 cup dried cannellini beans

1 small garlic clove, crushed

1 bunch scallions,
chopped roughly

handful of fresh mint leaves

2 tbsp sesame seed paste

2 tbsp olive oil

1 tsp ground cumin

1 tsp ground coriander

lemon juice

salt and pepper

sprigs of fresh mint, to garnish

TO SERVE

fresh vegetable crudités,
such as cauliflower florets,
carrots, cucumber, radishes,
and bell peppers

1 Soak the cannellini beans overnight in plenty of cold water.

2 Rinse and drain the beans, put them into a large saucepan, and cover them with cold water. Bring to a boil and boil rapidly for 10 minutes. Reduce the heat, cover, and simmer until tender.

3 Drain the beans and transfer to a bowl or food processor. Add the garlic, scallions, mint, sesame seed paste, and olive oil.

4 Blend the mixture for about 15 seconds, or mash well by hand, until smooth.

5 Transfer the mixture to a bowl and season with cumin, ground coriander, lemon juice, salt and pepper, according to taste. Mix well, cover, and leave in a cool place for 30 minutes to allow the flavors to develop.

6 Spoon the dip into serving bowls, garnish with sprigs of fresh mint, and surround with vegetable crudités.

Crispy Potato Skins

Potato skins are always a favorite. Prepare the skins in advance and warm through before serving with the salad fillings.

Serves 4

4 large baking potatoes

2 tbsp vegetable oil

4 tsp salt

$^2/_3$ cup sour cream and

2 tbsp chopped chives, to serve

BEAN SPROUT SALAD

$1^3/_4$ ounces bean sprouts

1 celery stick, sliced

1 orange, peeled
and segmented

1 red eating apple, chopped

$^1/_2$ red bell pepper, chopped

1 tbsp chopped parsley

1 tbsp light soy sauce

1 tbsp clear honey

1 small garlic clove, crushed

BEAN FILLING

$1^1/_2$ cups canned,
mixed beans, drained

1 onion, halved and sliced

1 tomato, chopped

2 scallions, chopped

2 tsp lemon juice

salt and pepper

1 Scrub the potatoes and put on a cookie sheet. Prick the potatoes all over with a fork and rub the oil and salt into the skin. Cook in a preheated oven at 400°F for 1 hour or until soft.

2 Cut the potatoes in half lengthwise and scoop out the flesh, leaving a $^1/_2$ inch thick shell. Put the shells, skin side uppermost, in the oven for 10 minutes until crisp.

3 Mix the ingredients for the bean sprout salad in a bowl, tossing in the soy, honey, and garlic to coat.

4 Mix the ingredients for the bean filling in a separate bowl.

5 Mix the sour cream and chives in another bowl.

6 Serve the potato skins hot, with the two salad fillings and the sour cream and chives.

Mixed Bean Pâté

This is a really quick starter to prepare if canned beans are used.
Choose a wide variety of beans for color and flavor or use a can of mixed beans.

Serves 4
14 ounce can mixed beans, drained
2 tbsp olive oil
juice of 1 lemon
2 garlic cloves, crushed
1 tbsp chopped fresh cilantro
2 scallions, chopped
salt and pepper
shredded scallions, to garnish

1 Rinse the beans under cold running water and drain well.

2 Transfer the beans to a food processor or blender. Alternatively, place in a bowl and mash with a fork or potato masher.

3 Add the olive oil, lemon juice, garlic, cilantro, and scallions and blend until fairly smooth. Season with salt and pepper to taste.

4 Transfer the pâté to a serving bowl and chill for at least 30 minutes. Garnish with shredded scallions and serve.

COOK'S TIP

Serve the pâté with warm pita bread or granary toast.

Onions à la Grecque

This is a well-known method of cooking vegetables and is perfect
with shallots or onions, served with a crisp salad.

Serves 4
1 pound shallots
3 tbsp olive oil
3 tbsp clear honey
2 tbsp garlic wine vinegar
3 tbsp dry white wine
1 tbsp tomato paste
2 celery stalks, sliced
2 tomatoes, seeded and chopped
chopped celery leaves, to garnish

1 Peel the shallots. Heat the oil in a
large saucepan and cook the shallots,
stirring, for 3–5 minutes or until they
begin to brown.

2 Add the honey and cook for a
further 30 seconds over a high heat,
then add the vinegar and wine,
stirring well.

3 Stir in the tomato paste celery, and
tomatoes and bring the mixture to the
boil. Cook over a high heat for 5–6
minutes. Season with salt and pepper
to taste and leave to cool slightly.

4 Garnish with chopped celery leaves
and serve warm or cold from the
refrigerator.

COOK'S VARIATION

Use button mushrooms instead
of the shallots and fennel instead
of the celery for another
great starter.

Bell Peppers with Rosemary Baste

The flavor of broiled or roasted bell peppers is very different
from when they are eaten raw, so do try them cooked in this way.

Serves 4
4 tbsp olive oil
finely grated rind of 1 lemon
4 tbsp lemon juice
1 tbsp balsamic vinegar
1 tbsp crushed fresh rosemary, or 1 tsp dried rosemary
2 red bell peppers, halved, cored, and deseeded
2 yellow bell peppers, halved, cored, and deseeded
2 tbsp pine nuts
salt and pepper
sprigs of fresh rosemary, to garnish

1 Mix together the olive oil, lemon rind, lemon juice, vinegar, and rosemary. Season with salt and pepper to taste.

2 Place the bell peppers, skin-side uppermost, on the rack of a broiler pan lined with foil. Brush the rosemary baste over the bell peppers.

3 Cook the bell peppers under a preheated broiler until the skin begins to char, basting frequently with the rosemary baste. Remove from the heat, cover with foil to trap the steam, and leave for 5 minutes.

4 Meanwhile, scatter the pine nuts onto the broiler rack and toast them lightly.

5 Peel the bell peppers, slice them into strips, and place them in a warmed serving dish.

6 Sprinkle the pine nuts over the bell peppers and drizzle with any remaining rosemary baste. Garnish with sprigs of fresh rosemary and serve at once.

COOK'S TIP

Rosemary contains oil of camphor, which gives an aromatic flavor.

Lentil Pâté

Red lentils are used in this spicy recipe for speed as they do not require pre-soaking.
If you have other lentils, soak and pre-cook them and use instead of the red lentils.

Serves 4
1 tbsp vegetable oil, plus extra for greasing
1 onion, chopped
2 garlic cloves, crushed
1 tsp garam masala
$\frac{1}{2}$ tsp ground coriander
1$\frac{1}{4}$ cups vegetable stock
$\frac{2}{3}$ cup red lentils
1 small egg
2 tbsp milk
2 tbsp mango chutney
2 tbsp chopped parsley
chopped parsley, to garnish
salad leaves and warm toast, to serve

1 Heat the oil in a large saucepan and sauté the onion and garlic for 2–3 minutes, stirring. Add the garam masala and ground coriander and cook for a further 30 seconds.

2 Stir in the stock and lentils and bring the mixture to a boil. Reduce the heat and simmer for 20 minutes until the lentils are cooked and softened. Remove the pan from the heat and drain off any excess moisture.

3 Put the mixture in a food processor and add the egg, milk, mango chutney, and parsley. Blend for 20 seconds until smooth.

4 Grease and line the base of a 1 pound loaf pan and spoon the mixture into the pan, levelling the surface with the back of a spoon. Cover and cook in a preheated oven at 400°F for 40–45 minutes or until firm to the touch.

5 Allow the pâté to cool in the pan for 20 minutes, then transfer to the refrigerator to cool completely.

6 Turn out the pâté onto a serving plate, slice, and garnish with chopped parsley. Serve with salad leaves and warm toast.

COOK'S VARIATION

Use other spices, such as chili powder or Chinese five-spice powder, to flavor the pâté and add tomato relish or chili relish instead of the mango chutney, if you prefer.

Roasted Vegetables on Muffins

Roasted vegetables are delicious and attractive. Served on warm muffins
with a herb sauce, they are unbeatable.

Serves 4
1 red onion, cut into eight
1 eggplant, halved and sliced
1 yellow bell pepper, sliced
1 zucchini, sliced
4 tbsp olive oil
1 tbsp garlic vinegar
2 tbsp vermouth
2 garlic cloves, crushed
1 tbsp chopped thyme
2 tsp light brown sugar
4 muffins, halved
salt and pepper
fresh herbs, to garnish
SAUCE
2 tbsp butter
1 tbsp flour
$2/3$ cup milk
$1/3$ cup vegetable stock
$3/4$ cup vegetarian Cheddar, grated
1 tsp wholegrain mustard
3 tbsp chopped mixed herbs

1 Arrange the vegetables in a shallow ovenproof dish. Mix the oil, vinegar, vermouth, garlic, thyme, and sugar together and pour over the vegetables. Leave to marinate for 1 hour.

2 Transfer the vegetables to a cookie sheet. Cook in a pre-heated oven at 400°F for about 20–25 minutes or until softened.

3 Meanwhile, make the sauce. Melt the butter in a small pan and add the flour. Cook for 1 minute and remove from the heat. Stir in the milk and stock and return the pan to the heat. Bring to a boil, stirring, until thickened. Stir in the cheese, mustard, and mixed herbs and season well.

4 Preheat the broiler to high. Cut the muffins in half and broil for 2–3 minutes until golden brown, then remove and arrange on a serving plate.

5 Spoon the roasted vegetables onto the muffins and pour the sauce over the top. Garnish with fresh herbs and serve immediately.

Mushroom & Garlic Soufflés

These individual soufflés are very impressive starters, but must be cooked just before serving to prevent them sinking.

Serves 4
4 tbsp butter
2³/₄ ounces flat mushrooms, chopped
2 tsp lime juice
2 garlic cloves, crushed
2 tbsp chopped marjoram
3 tbsp all-purpose flour
1 cup milk
salt and pepper
2 eggs, separated

4 Add the sauce to the mushroom mixture, mixing well, and beat in the egg yolks.

5 Whisk the egg whites until peaking and fold into the mushroom mixture until fully incorporated.

6 Divide the mixture between the four soufflé dishes. Place the dishes on a cookie sheet and cook in a preheated oven at 400°F for 8–10 minutes or until the soufflés have risen and are cooked through. Serve immediately.

1 Lightly grease the inside of four ¼ pint individual soufflé dishes with a little butter.

2 Melt 2 tbsp of the butter in a skillet. Add the mushrooms, lime juice, and garlic and sauté for 2–3 minutes. Remove the mushroom mixture from the skillet with a slotted spoon and transfer to a mixing bowl. Stir in the marjoram.

3 Melt the remaining butter in a pan. Add the flour and cook for 1 minute, then remove from the heat. Stir in the milk and return to the heat. Bring to a boil, stirring until thickened.

COOK'S TIP

Insert a skewer into the center of the soufflés to test if they are cooked through—it should come out clean. If not, cook for a few minutes longer, but do not overcook otherwise they will become rubbery.

Eggplant Timbale

This is a great way to serve pasta as a starter, wrapped in an eggplant mold. It looks really impressive yet it is so easy to make.

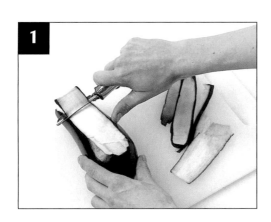

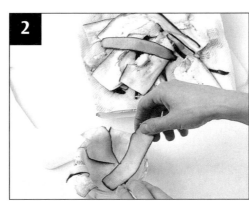

Serves 4
1 large eggplant
¹/₂ cup macaroni
1 tbsp vegetable oil
1 onion, chopped
2 garlic cloves, crushed
2 tbsp drained canned corn
2 tbsp frozen peas, thawed
3¹/₂ ounces spinach
¹/₄ cup vegetarian Cheddar, grated
1 egg, beaten
8 ounces canned, chopped tomatoes
1 tbsp chopped basil
salt and pepper

SAUCE
4 tbsp olive oil
2 tbsp white wine vinegar
2 garlic cloves, crushed
3 tbsp chopped basil
1 tbsp superfine sugar

1 Cut the eggplant lengthwise into thin strips, using a potato peeler. Place in a bowl of salted, boiling water and leave to stand for 3–4 minutes. Drain well.

2 Lightly grease four ¹/₄ pint individual ramekin dishes and use the eggplant slices to line the dishes, leaving 1 inch of eggplant overlapping.

3 Cook the pasta in a pan of boiling water for 8–10 minutes or until "al dente". Drain. Heat the oil in a pan and sauté the onion and garlic for 2–3 minutes. Stir in the corn and peas and remove from the heat.

4 Blanch the spinach, drain well, chop, and reserve. Add the pasta to the onion mixture with the cheese, egg, tomatoes, and basil. Season and mix. Half-fill each ramekin with some of the pasta. Spoon the spinach on top and then the remaining pasta mixture. Fold the eggplant over the pasta filling to cover. Put the ramekins in a roasting pan half-filled with boiling water, cover, and cook in a preheated oven at 350°F for 20–25 minutes or until set. Meanwhile, heat the ingredients for the sauce in a pan. Turn out the ramekins and serve with the sauce.

Carrot, Fennel, & Potato Medley

This is a colorful dish of shredded vegetables in a fresh garlic and honey dressing.
It is delicious served with crusty bread to mop up the dressing.

Serves 4
2 tbsp olive oil
1 potato, cut into thin strips
1 fennel bulb, cut into thin strips
2 carrots, grated
1 red onion, cut into thin strips
chopped chives and fennel fronds, to garnish
DRESSING
3 tbsp olive oil
1 tbsp garlic wine vinegar
1 garlic clove, crushed
1 tsp Dijon mustard
2 tsp clear honey
salt and pepper

1 Heat the oil in a skillet and cook the potato and fennel slices for 2–3 minutes until beginning to brown. Remove with a slotted spoon and drain on paper towels.

2 Arrange the carrot, red onion, and potato and fennel on a serving platter.

3 Mix the dressing ingredients together and pour over the vegetables. Toss well and sprinkle with chopped chives and fennel fronds.

COOK'S VARIATION

Use mixed, broiled bell peppers or shredded leeks in this dish for variety, or add bean sprouts and a segmented orange, if you prefer.

Light Meals

The ability to rustle up a quick light meal can be very important in our busy lives. Sometimes we may not feel like eating a full-scale meal but nevertheless want something appetizing and satisfying. Or, if lunch or dinner is going to be served late, then we may want something to tide us over.

Whatever the occasion, you're guaranteed to find a mouthwatering collection of recipes in this chapter. The recipes cater to all tastes and times of day. Many of the recipes can be prepared way

ahead of time and will not detain you in the kitchen for too long.

With such a versatile selection of recipes to choose from, using a wide range of exciting flavors and ingredients, you will easily find something to satisfy your hunger, with hardly a sandwich in sight!

Roman Focaccia

Roman focaccia makes a delicious snack on its own or
serve it with salad for a quick supper.

Makes 16 squares
$^1/_4$ ounce dried yeast
1 tsp sugar
1$^1/_4$ cups hand-hot water
1 pound strong flour
2 tsp salt
3 tbsp rosemary, chopped
2 tbsp olive oil
1 pound mixed red and white onions, sliced into rings
4 garlic cloves, sliced
fresh rosemary, to garnish

1 Place the yeast and sugar in a small bowl with 8 tbsp of the water. Leave to ferment in a warm place for 15 minutes.

2 Mix the flour with the salt in a large bowl.

3 Add the yeast mixture, half of the rosemary, and the remaining water and mix to form a smooth dough. Knead the dough for 4 minutes.

4 Cover the dough with oiled plastic wrap and leave to rise for 30 minutes or until doubled in size.

5 Meanwhile, heat the oil in a large pan. Add the onions and garlic and fry for 5 minutes or until softened. Cover the pan and continue to cook for a further 7–8 minutes or until the onions are lightly caramelized.

6 Remove the plastic wrap from the dough and knead the dough again for 1–2 minutes.

7 Roll the dough out to form a square shape. The dough should be no more than $^1/_4$ inch thick because it will rise during cooking.

8 Place the dough onto a large cookie sheet, pushing out the edges until even.

9 Spread the caramelized onions over the dough, and sprinkle with the remaining rosemary. Bake the focaccia in a preheated oven at 400°F for 25–30 minutes or until golden. Cut the Roman focaccia into 16 squares, garnish with fresh rosemary, and serve immediately.

Vegetable Samosas

These Indian snacks are perfect for a quick or light meal.
Served with a salad they can be made in advance and frozen for ease.

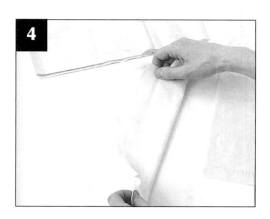

Makes 12
FILLING
2 tbsp vegetable oil
1 onion, chopped
$^1/_2$ tsp ground coriander
$^1/_2$ tsp ground cumin
pinch of turmeric
$^1/_2$ tsp ground ginger
$^1/_2$ tsp garam masala
1 garlic clove, crushed
8 ounces potatoes, diced
1 cup frozen peas, thawed
$5^1/_2$ ounces spinach, chopped
PASTRY
12 sheets filo pastry
oil, for deep-frying

1 To make the filling, heat the oil in a skillet and sauté the onion for 1–2 minutes, stirring until softened. Stir in all of the spices and garlic and cook for 1 minute.

2 Add the potatoes and cook over a gentle heat for 5 minutes, stirring until they begin to soften.

3 Stir in the peas and spinach and cook for a further 3–4 minutes.

4 Lay the filo pastry sheets out on a clean counter and fold each sheet in half lengthwise.

5 Place 2 tbsp of the vegetable filling at one end of each folded pastry sheet. Fold over one corner to make a triangle. Continue folding in this way to make a triangular packet and seal

the edges with water. Repeat with the remaining pastry and filling.

6 Heat the oil for deep-frying to 350°F or until a cube of bread browns in 30 seconds. Fry the samosas, in batches, for 1–2 minutes until golden. Drain on absorbent paper towels and

keep warm while cooking the remainder. Serve.

COOK'S TIP

Serve with a yogurt sauce (see page 43) and a salad.

Bean Curd Stuffed Mushrooms

Use large open-cap mushrooms for this recipe
for their flavor and suitability for filling.

Serves 4
8 open-cap mushrooms
1 tbsp olive oil
1 small leek, chopped
1 celery stick, chopped
3¹/₂ ounces firm bean curd, diced
1 zucchini, chopped
1 carrot, chopped
1 cup whole wheat bread crumbs
2 tbsp chopped basil
1 tbsp tomato paste
2 tbsp pine nuts
³/₄ cup vegetarian Cheddar cheese, grated
²/₃ cup vegetable stock
salt and pepper
green salad, to serve

6 Cook in a preheated oven at 425°F
for 20 minutes or until cooked
through and the cheese has melted.
Remove the mushrooms from the
dish and serve immediately with a
green salad.

COOK'S TIP

Vary the vegetables used for flavor
and color or according to those you
have available.

1 Remove the stalks from the
mushrooms and chop finely.

2 Heat the oil in a skillet. Add the
chopped mushroom stalks, leek,
celery, bean curd, zucchini, and
carrot, and cook for 3–4 minutes,
stirring.

3 Stir in the bread crumbs, basil,
tomato paste, and pine nuts. Season
with salt and pepper to taste.

4 Spoon the mixture into the
mushrooms and top with the cheese.

5 Place the mushrooms in a shallow
ovenproof dish and pour the
vegetable stock around them.

Ricotta & Spinach Packets

Ricotta and spinach make a great flavor combination,
especially when encased in light puff-pastry packets.

Serves 4
12 ounces spinach
trimmed and washed thoroughly
2 tbsp butter
1 small onion, chopped finely
1 tsp green peppercorns
1 pound puff pastry
1 cup Ricotta
1 egg, beaten
salt
sprigs of fresh herbs, to garnish
fresh vegetables, to serve

1 Pack the spinach into a large saucepan. Add a little salt and a very small amount of water and cook until wilted. Drain well, cool, and then squeeze out any excess moisture with the back of a spoon. Chop roughly.

2 Melt the butter in a small saucepan and fry the onion gently until softened, but not browned. Add the green peppercorns and cook for 2 minutes. Remove from the heat, add the spinach, and mix together.

3 Roll out the puff pastry thinly on a lightly floured work surface and cut into 4 squares, each 7 inches across. Place a quarter of the spinach mixture in the center of each square and top with a quarter of the cheese.

4 Brush a little beaten egg around the edges of the pastry squares and bring the corners together to form packets. Press the edges together to seal. Lift the packets onto a greased cookie sheet, brush with beaten egg, and bake in a preheated oven at 400°F for 20–25 minutes, until risen and golden.

5 Serve hot, garnished with sprigs of fresh herbs and accompanied by fresh vegetables.

Garlic Mushrooms on Toast

This is so simple to prepare and looks great if you use a variety of mushrooms for shape and texture. Cooked in garlic butter, they are simply irresistible.

Serves 4
6 tbsp vegetarian margarine
2 garlic cloves, crushed
12 ounces mixed mushrooms, such as open-cap, button, oyster, and shiitake, sliced
1 tbsp chopped parsley
8 slices French bread
salt and pepper

1 Melt the margarine in a skillet. Add the garlic and cook for 30 seconds, stirring.

2 Add the mushrooms and cook for 5 minutes, turning occasionally.

3 Meanwhile, toast the French bread slices under a preheated medium broiler for 2–3 minutes, turning once. Transfer the toasts to a serving plate.

4 Toss the parsley into the mushrooms, mixing well, and spoon the mixture over the bread. Serve immediately.

COOK'S TIP

Add seasonings, such as curry powder or chili powder, to the mushrooms for extra flavor, if liked.

Mixed Bean Pan-Fry

Fresh green beans have a wonderful flavor that is hard to beat.
If you cannot find fresh beans, use thawed, frozen beans instead.

Serves 4
12 ounces mixed green beans, such as green and fava beans
2 tbsp vegetable oil
2 garlic cloves, crushed
1 red onion, halved and sliced
8 ounces firm marinated bean curd, diced
1 tbsp lemon juice
$1/2$ tsp turmeric
1 tsp ground mixed spice
$2/3$ cup vegetable stock
2 tsp sesame seeds

1 Trim and chop the green beans. Set aside until required.

2 Heat the oil in a skillet and sauté the garlic and onion for 2 minutes, stirring well.

3 Add the bean curd and cook for 2–3 minutes until just beginning to brown.

4 Add the green beans and fava beans. Stir in the lemon juice, turmeric, mixed spice, and stock and bring to a boil. Reduce the heat and simmer for 5–7 minutes or until the beans are tender. Sprinkle with sesame seeds and serve immediately.

COOK'S VARIATION

Use smoked bean curd instead of marinated bean curd for an alternative flavor.

Bulgar-Filled Eggplants

In this recipe, eggplants are filled with a spicy bulgar wheat
and vegetable stuffing for a delicious light meal.

Serves 4
4 medium eggplants
salt
3/4 cup bulgar wheat
1 1/4 cups boiling water
3 tbsp olive oil
2 garlic cloves, crushed
2 tbsp pine nuts
1/2 tsp turmeric
1 tsp chili powder
2 celery sticks, chopped
4 scallions, chopped
1 carrot, grated
1 3/4 ounces button mushrooms, chopped
2 tbsp raisins
2 tbsp chopped fresh cilantro
green salad, to serve

1 Cut the eggplants in half
lengthwise and scoop out the flesh
with a teaspoon. Chop the flesh and
set aside. Rub the insides of the
eggplants with a little salt and leave to
stand for 20 minutes to extract the
bitter juices.

2 Meanwhile, put the bulgar wheat
in a mixing bowl and pour the boiling
water over the top. Leave to stand for
20 minutes or until the water has
been absorbed.

3 Heat the oil in a skillet. Add the
garlic, nuts, turmeric, chili powder,
celery, scallions, carrot, mushrooms,
and raisins and cook for 2–3
minutes.

4 Stir in the reserved eggplant flesh
and cook for a further 2–3 minutes.
Add the cilantro, mixing well.

5 Remove the pan from the heat and
stir in the bulgar wheat. Rinse the
eggplant shells under cold water and
pat dry with absorbent paper towels.

6 Spoon the bulgar filling into the
eggplants and place in a roasting pan.
Pour in a little boiling water and cook
in a preheated oven at 350°F for
15–20 minutes.

7 Remove the eggplants from the pan
and serve hot with a green salad.

Creamy Mushroom Vol-au-Vent

A simple mixture of creamy, tender mushrooms filling a crisp, rich pastry case,
this dish will make an impression at any dinner party.

Serves 4
1 pound 2 ounces puff pastry, thawed if frozen
1 egg, beaten, for glazing
FILLING
2 tbsp butter or vegetarian margarine
1 pound 10 ounces mixed mushrooms such as open-cap, field, button, chestnut, shiitake, and pied de mouton, sliced
6 tbsp dry white wine
4 tbsp heavy cream
2 tbsp chopped fresh chervil
salt and pepper
sprigs of fresh chervil, to garnish

1 Roll out the pastry on a lightly floured counter to form an 8 inch square.

2 Using a sharp knife, mark a square 1 inch from the pastry edge, cutting halfway through the pastry.

3 Score the top of the square in a diagonal pattern. Knock up the edges with a kitchen knife and place on a cookie sheet. Brush the top with beaten egg, taking care not to let the egg run into the cut edges. Bake in a preheated oven at 425°F for 35 minutes.

4 Cut out the central square. Scoop out the soft pastry inside the case and discard, leaving the base intact. Return to the oven, together with the central square, for about 10 minutes.

5 To make the filling, melt the butter in a skillet and stir-fry the mushrooms for 3 minutes.

6 Add the wine and cook for 10 minutes, stirring occasionally, until the mushrooms have softened. Stir in the cream, chervil, and seasoning.

7 Spoon the filling into the pastry case. Top with the pastry square, garnish, and serve.

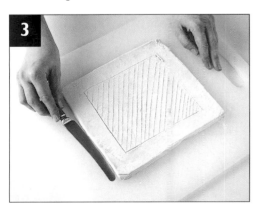

Potato, Bell Pepper, & Mushroom Hash

This is a quick one-pan dish which is ideal for a quick snack. Packed with color and flavor it is very versatile and you can add any other vegetable you have to hand.

Serves 4

$1^1/_2$ pounds potatoes, cubed

1 tbsp olive oil

2 garlic cloves, crushed

1 green bell pepper, cubed

1 yellow bell pepper, cubed

3 tomatoes, diced

$2^3/_4$ ounces button mushrooms, halved

1 tbsp vegetarian Worcester sauce

2 tbsp chopped basil

salt and pepper

fresh basil sprigs, to garnish

warm, crusty bread, to serve

1 Cook the potatoes in a saucepan of boiling, salted water for 7–8 minutes. Drain well and reserve.

2 Heat the oil in a large, heavy-based skillet and cook the potatoes for 8–10 minutes, stirring until browned.

3 Add the garlic and bell peppers and cook for 2–3 minutes. Stir in the tomatoes and mushrooms and cook, stirring, for 5–6 minutes.

4 Stir in the vegetarian Worcester sauce and basil and season well. Garnish and serve with crusty bread.

COOK'S TIP

Most brands of Worcester sauce contain anchovies so make sure you choose a vegetarian variety.

Leek & Sun-dried Tomato Timbales

Angel-hair pasta, known as cappellini, is mixed with fried leeks, sun-dried tomatoes, fresh oregano, and beaten eggs, and baked in ramekins.

Serves 4

3 ounces angel-hair pasta (cappellini)

2 tbsp butter

1 tbsp olive oil

1 large leek, sliced finely

$\frac{1}{2}$ cup sun-dried tomatoes in oil, drained and chopped

1 tbsp chopped fresh oregano or 1 tsp dried oregano

2 eggs, beaten

generous $\frac{1}{3}$ cup light cream

1 tbsp freshly grated Parmesan

salt and pepper

sprigs of oregano, to garnish

lettuce leaves, to serve

TOMATO SAUCE

1 small onion, chopped finely

1 small garlic clove, crushed

12 ounces tomatoes, peeled and chopped

1 tsp mixed dried Italian herbs

4 tbsp dry white wine

1 Cook the pasta in a pan of boiling, salted water for about 3 minutes until "al dente" (just tender). Drain and rinse with cold water to cool quickly.

2 Meanwhile, heat the butter and oil in a skillet. Gently fry the leek until softened, about 5–6 minutes. Add the sun-dried tomatoes and oregano and cook for a further 2 minutes. Remove from the heat.

3 Add the leek mixture to the pasta. Stir in the beaten eggs, cream, and Parmesan and season.

4 Divide the mixture between 4 greased ramekins. Place in a roasting pan with enough warm water to come halfway up their sides. Bake in a preheated oven at 350°F for 30 minutes, or until set.

5 To make the sauce, fry the onion and garlic until softened. Add the tomatoes, herbs, and wine. Cover and cook for 20 minutes until pulpy. Blend in a food processor or press through a sieve until smooth.

6 Run a knife around the edge of the ramekin dishes, then turn out the timbales onto 4 serving plates. Pour over a little sauce, garnish, and serve.

Marinated Broiled Fennel

Fennel has a wonderful aniseed flavor which is ideal for broiling or barbecuing.
Marinated in lime, garlic, oil, and mustard, this recipe is really delicious.

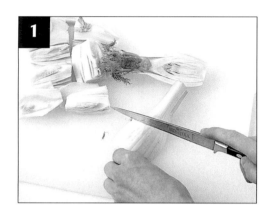

Serves 4
2 fennel bulbs
1 red bell pepper, cut into large cubes
1 lime, cut into eight wedges
MARINADE
2 tbsp lime juice
4 tbsp olive oil
2 garlic cloves, crushed
1 tsp wholegrain mustard
1 tbsp chopped thyme
fennel fronds, to garnish
crisp salad, to serve

1 Cut each of the fennel bulbs into eight pieces and place in a shallow dish. Mix in the bell peppers.

2 To make the marinade, combine the lime juice, oil, garlic, mustard, and thyme. Pour the marinade over the fennel and bell peppers and leave to marinate for 1 hour.

3 Thread the fennel and bell peppers onto wooden skewers with the lime wedges. Preheat a broiler to medium and broil the kabobs for 10 minutes, turning and basting with the marinade. Transfer to serving plates, garnish with fennel fronds, and serve with a crisp salad.

COOK'S TIP

Soak the skewers in water for 20 minutes before using to prevent them from burning during cooking.

Scrambled Bean Curd on Toast

This is a delicious dish which would also
serve as a light lunch or supper.

Serves 4
6 tbsp vegetarian margarine
1 pound marinated, firm bean curd
1 red onion, chopped
1 red bell pepper, chopped
4 ciabatta rolls, halved
2 tbsp chopped mixed herbs
salt and pepper
fresh herbs, to garnish

1 Melt the margarine in a skillet and crumble the bean curd into the pan.

2 Add the onion and bell pepper and cook for 3–4 minutes, stirring occasionally.

3 Meanwhile, toast the ciabatta rolls under a hot broiler for 2–3 minutes, turning once. Remove and transfer to a serving plate.

4 Add the herbs to the bean curd mixture, combine, and season.

5 Spoon the bean curd mixture onto the toast and garnish with fresh herbs. Serve at once.

COOK'S TIP

Marinated bean curd adds extra flavor to this dish. Smoked bean curd could be used in its place.

Refried Beans with Tortillas

Refried beans are a classic Mexican dish and are usually served as an accompaniment.
They are, however, delicious when served with warm tortillas and a quick onion relish.

Serves 4
BEANS
2 tbsp olive oil
1 onion, finely chopped
3 garlic cloves, crushed
1 green chili, chopped
14 ounce can red kidney beans, drained
14 ounce can pinto beans, drained
2 tbsp chopped cilantro
$^2/_3$ cup vegetable stock
8 wheat tortillas
$^1/_4$ cup vegetarian Cheddar cheese, grated
salt and pepper
RELISH
4 scallions, chopped
1 red onion, chopped
1 green chili, chopped
1 tbsp garlic wine vinegar
1 tsp superfine sugar
1 tomato, chopped

1 Heat the oil for the beans in a large skillet. Add the onion and sauté for 3–5 minutes until softened. Add the garlic and chili and cook for another minute.

2 Mash the beans with a potato masher and stir into the pan with the cilantro.

3 Stir in the stock and cook the beans, stirring, for 5 minutes until soft and pulpy.

4 Place the tortillas on a cookie sheet and heat through in a warm oven for

1–2 minutes. Mix the relish ingredients together.

5 Spoon the beans into a serving dish and top with the cheese. Season well. Roll the tortillas and serve with the relish and beans.

COOK'S TIP

Add a little more liquid to the beans when they are cooking if they begin to catch on the bottom of the skillet.

Cauliflower Roulade

A light-as-air mixture of eggs and vegetables produces a stylish vegetarian dish that can be enjoyed hot or cold.

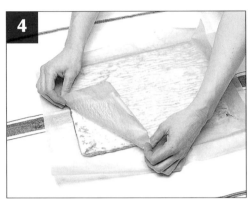

Serves 6

1 small cauliflower, divided into florets
4 eggs, separated
$^3/_4$ cup Cheddar, grated
$^1/_4$ cup cottage cheese
large pinch of grated nutmeg
$^1/_2$ tsp mustard powder
salt and pepper

FILLING

1 bunch watercress, trimmed
$^1/_4$ cup butter
$^1/_4$ cup flour
$^3/_4$ cup natural yogurt
$^1/_4$ cup Cheddar, grated
$^1/_4$ cup cottage cheese

1 Line a Swiss roll pan with baking parchment. Steam the cauliflower until just tender, then drain. Put the cauliflower in a food processor and finely process, or chop finely and push through a sieve using the back of a spoon.

2 Beat the egg yolks, then stir in the cauliflower, $^1/_2$ cup of the Cheddar, and the cottage cheese. Season with nutmeg, mustard, and salt and pepper to taste. Whisk the egg whites until stiff but not dry, then fold into the cauliflower, using a metal spoon. Spread the mixture in the prepared pan and bake in a preheated oven at 400°F for 20–25 minutes, until risen and golden.

3 For the filling, chop the watercress, reserving a few sprigs for garnish. Melt the butter in a small pan, add

the watercress and cook for 3 minutes, stirring, until wilted. Blend in the flour, then stir in the yogurt, and simmer for 2 minutes. Stir in the cheeses.

4 Turn out the roulade onto a damp dish cloth covered with baking parchment. Peel off the paper and leave

for 1 minute to allow the steam to escape. Roll up the roulade, including a new sheet of paper, starting from one narrow end. Unroll the roulade, spread the filling to within 1 inch of the edges, and roll up. Transfer to a cookie sheet, sprinkle on the Cheddar, and return to the oven for 5 minutes. Serve.

Falafel

This is a very tasty, well-known Middle Eastern dish of small garbanzo bean based balls, spiced and deep-fried. They are delicious hot with a crisp tomato salad.

Serves 4
6 cups canned garbanzo beans, drained
1 red onion, chopped
3 garlic cloves, crushed
3¹/₂ ounces whole wheat bread
2 small red chilies
1 tsp ground cumin
1 tsp ground coriander
¹/₂ tsp turmeric
1 tbsp chopped cilantro, plus extra to garnish
1 egg, beaten
1 cup whole wheat bread crumbs
vegetable oil, for deep-frying
salt and pepper

3 Heat the oil for deep-frying to 350°F or until a cube of bread browns in 30 seconds. Fry the falafel, in batches, for 2–3 minutes until crisp

and browned. Remove from the oil with a slotted spoon and dry on absorbent paper towels. Garnish with cilantro and serve.

1 Put the garbanzo beans, onion, garlic, bread, chilies, spices, and cilantro in a food processor and blend for 30 seconds. Stir and season with salt and pepper to taste. Remove the mixture from the food processor and, using a teaspoon, shape into walnut-sized balls.

2 Place the beaten egg in a shallow bowl. Dip the balls into the egg to coat and then roll them in the bread crumbs, shaking off any excess.

COOK'S TIP

Serve the falafel with a cilantro and yogurt sauce. Mix ²/₃ cup natural yogurt with 2 tbsp chopped cilantro and 1 crushed garlic clove.

Ciabatta Vegetable Rolls

Sandwiches are always a welcome snack but can be quite mundane.
These crisp ciabatta rolls filled with roasted bell peppers and cheese are irresistible
and will always be a popular light meal.

Serves 4
4 ciabatta rolls
2 tbsp olive oil
1 garlic clove crushed
FILLING
1 red bell pepper
1 green bell pepper
1 yellow bell pepper
4 radishes, sliced
1 bunch watercress
8 tbsp cream cheese

1 Halve the ciabatta rolls. Heat the oil and garlic in a pan. Pour the garlic and oil mixture over the cut surfaces of the rolls and leave to stand.

2 Halve the bell peppers and place, skin side uppermost, on a broiler rack. Cook under a hot broiler for 8–10 minutes until just beginning to char. Remove the bell peppers from the broiler, peel, and slice thinly.

3 Arrange the radish slices on one half of each roll with a few watercress leaves. Spoon the cream cheese on top. Pile the bell peppers on top of the cream cheese and top with the other half of the roll. Serve.

COOK'S TIP

Allow the bell peppers to cool slightly before filling the roll, otherwise the cheese will melt.

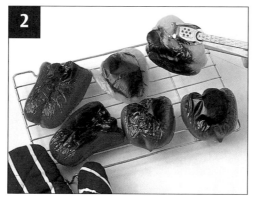

Bean Curd & Vegetable Mini Kabobs

Cubes of smoked bean curd are speared on bamboo satay sticks with crisp vegetables, basted with lemon juice and olive oil, and then broiled.

Serves 6
10$\frac{1}{2}$ ounces smoked bean curd, cut into cubes
1 large red and 1 large yellow bell pepper, seeded and cut into small squares
6 ounces button mushrooms, wiped
1 small zucchini, sliced
finely grated rind and juice of 1 lemon
3 tbsp olive oil
1 tbsp chopped fresh parsley
1 tsp superfine sugar
salt and pepper
fresh herbs, to garnish
SAUCE
1 cup cashew nuts
1 tbsp butter
1 garlic clove, crushed
1 shallot, chopped finely
1 tsp ground coriander
1 tsp ground cumin
1 tbsp superfine sugar
1 tbsp shredded coconut
$\frac{2}{3}$ cup natural yogurt

1 Thread the bean curd cubes, bell peppers, mushrooms, and zucchini onto bamboo satay sticks. Arrange in a shallow dish.

2 Mix together the lemon rind and juice, oil, parsley, and sugar. Season with salt and pepper. Pour over the kabobs, brushing them with the mixture. Leave for 10 minutes.

3 To make the sauce, scatter the cashew nuts onto a cookie sheet and toast until browned.

4 Melt the butter in a saucepan and cook the garlic and shallot gently until softened. Transfer to a blender or food processor, add the cashew nuts, ground coriander, cumin, sugar, coconut, and yogurt and blend until combined, about 15 seconds. Alternatively, chop the cashew nuts very finely by hand and mix with the remaining ingredients.

5 Place the kabobs under a preheated broiler and cook, turning and basting frequently with the lemon juice mixture, until lightly browned.

6 Transfer the kabobs to serving plates and garnish with fresh herbs. Serve with the cashew nut sauce.

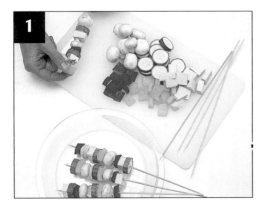

Calzone with Sun-dried Tomatoes & Vegetables

These pizza base packets are great for making in advance and freezing—they can be defrosted when required for a quick snack.

Makes 4
DOUGH
3¹/₂ cups strong white flour
2 tsp easy-blend dried yeast
1 tsp superfine sugar
²/₃ cup vegetable stock
²/₃ cup sieved tomatoes
beaten egg
FILLING
1 tbsp vegetable oil
1 onion, chopped
1 garlic clove, crushed
2 tbsp chopped sun-dried tomatoes
3¹/₂ ounces spinach, chopped
3 tbsp canned and drained corn
1 ounce green beans, cut into three
1 tbsp tomato paste
1 tbsp chopped oregano
1³/₄ ounces Mozzarella cheese, sliced
salt and pepper

1 Sieve the flour into a bowl. Add the yeast and sugar and beat in the stock and sieved tomatoes to make a smooth dough.

2 Knead the dough on a lightly floured surface for 10 minutes. Place the dough in a clean, lightly oiled bowl and leave to rise in a warm place for 1 hour or until doubled in size.

3 Meanwhile, heat the oil for the filling in a skillet and sauté the onion for 2–3 minutes until softened. Stir in the garlic, tomatoes, spinach, corn, and beans and cook for a further

3–4 minutes, stirring. Add the tomato paste, oregano, and salt and pepper to taste.

4 Divide the risen dough into 4 equal portions and roll each onto a floured surface to form a 7 inch circle. Spoon a quarter of the filling onto one half of

each circle and top with cheese. Fold the dough over to encase the filling, sealing the edge with a fork. Glaze with beaten egg. Put the calzone on a lightly greased cookie sheet and cook in a preheated oven at 425°F for 25–30 minutes until risen and golden. Serve warm.

Spinach Frittata

A frittata is another word for a large, thick omelet.
This is an Italian dish which may be made with many flavorings.
Spinach is used as the main ingredient in this recipe for color and flavor.

Serves 4
1 pound spinach
2 tsp water
4 eggs, beaten
2 tbsp light cream
2 garlic cloves, crushed
$^3/_4$ cup canned corn, drained
1 celery stick, chopped
1 red chili, chopped
2 tomatoes, seeded and diced
2 tbsp olive oil
2 tbsp butter
$^1/_4$ cup pecan nut halves
2 tbsp grated Pecorino cheese
1 ounce Fontina cheese, cubed
a pinch of paprika

1 Cook the spinach in 2 teaspoons of water in a covered pan for 5 minutes. Drain thoroughly and pat dry on absorbent paper towels.

2 Beat the eggs in a bowl and stir in the spinach, cream, garlic, corn, celery, chili, and tomato.

3 Heat the oil and butter in an 8 inch heavy-based skillet.

COOK'S TIP

Be careful not to burn the underside of the frittata during the initial cooking stage—this is why it is important to use a heavy-based skillet. Add a little extra oil to the skillet when you turn the frittata over if required.

4 Spoon the egg mixture into the skillet and sprinkle with the pecan nut halves, Pecorino and Fontina cheeses, and paprika. Cook without stirring over a medium heat for 5–7 minutes or until the underside of the frittata is brown.

5 Put a large plate over the pan and invert carefully to turn out the frittata. Slide it back into the skillet and cook the other side for a further 2–3 minutes. Serve the frittata straight from the skillet or transfer to a serving plate.

Eggplant & Mushroom Satay

Broiled, skewered vegetables are served with a satay sauce.

Serves 4
2 eggplants, cut into 1 inch pieces
6 ounces small chestnut mushrooms

MARINADE

1 tsp cumin seeds
1 tsp coriander seeds
1 inch piece ginger root, grated
2 garlic cloves, crushed lightly
1/2 stalk lemon grass, chopped roughly
4 tbsp light soy sauce
8 tbsp sunflower oil
2 tbsp lemon juice

PEANUT SAUCE

1/2 tsp cumin seeds
1/2 tsp coriander seeds
3 garlic cloves
1 small onion, quartered
1 tbsp lemon juice
1 tsp salt
1/2 red chili, seeded and sliced
1/2 cup coconut milk
1 cup crunchy peanut butter
1 cup water

1 Thread the eggplants and mushrooms onto eight skewers.

2 To make the marinade, grind the cumin, coriander, ginger, garlic, and lemon grass together. Add to a wok or a skillet and stir-fry over a high heat until fragrant. Remove from the heat and add the remaining marinade ingredients.

3 Place the skewers in a non-porous dish and spoon the marinade over.

Leave to marinate for a minimum of 2 hours and up to 8 hours.

4 To make the sauce, grind together the cumin, coriander, and garlic. Purée the onion in a food processor, or chop finely by hand, then add to the cumin mixture. Add the remaining ingredients, except for the water.

Transfer to a pan and blend in the water. Bring to a boil and cook until thickened. Transfer to a serving bowl.

5 Place the skewers on a cookie sheet and cook under a hot broiler for 15–20 minutes. Brush with the marinade and turn once. Serve with the peanut sauce.

Vegetable Burgers

These spicy vegetable burgers are delicious, especially when served with the light oven fries.
Serve them in a warm bun or roll with radicchio leaves and red onion relish.

Serves 4
VEGETABLE BURGERS
3¹/₂ ounces spinach
1 tbsp olive oil
1 leek, chopped
2 garlic cloves, crushed
3¹/₂ ounces mushrooms, chopped
10¹/₂ ounces firm bean curd, chopped
1 tsp chili powder
1 tsp curry powder
1 tbsp chopped cilantro
2³/₄ ounces fresh whole wheat bread crumbs
1 tbsp olive oil
FRIES
2 large potatoes
2 tbsp flour
1 tsp chili powder
2 tbsp olive oil
burger bun or roll and salad, to serve

1 To make the burgers, cook the spinach in a little water for 2 minutes. Drain thoroughly and pat dry with absorbent paper towels.

2 Heat the oil in a skillet and sauté the leek and garlic for 2–3 minutes. Add the remaining ingredients except for the bread crumbs and cook for 5–7 minutes until the vegetables have softened. Toss in the spinach and cook for 1 minute.

3 Transfer the mixture to a food processor and blend for 30 seconds until almost smooth. Stir in the bread crumbs, mixing well, and leave until

cool enough to handle. Using floured hands, form the mixture into four equal-sized burgers. Leave to chill for 30 minutes.

4 To make the fries, cut the potatoes into thin wedges and cook in a pan of boiling water for 10 minutes. Drain and toss in the flour and chili. Lay

the fries on a cookie sheet and sprinkle with the oil. Cook in a preheated oven at 400°F for 30 minutes or until golden.

5 Meanwhile, heat 1 tbsp oil in a skillet and cook the burgers for 8–10 minutes, turning once. Serve with salad in a burger bun.

Spinach Pancakes

Serve these pancakes as a light lunch or supper dish, with a tomato and basil salad for a dramatic color contrast.

Makes 8–12 pancakes
³/₄ cup whole wheat flour
1 egg
²/₃ cup natural yogurt
3 tbsp water
1 tbsp vegetable oil, plus extra for frying
7 ounces frozen leaf spinach, defrosted and liquid zed
pinch of grated nutmeg
salt and pepper
lemon wedges and fresh cilantro sprigs, to garnish
FILLING
1 tbsp vegetable oil
3 scallions, thinly sliced
1 cup Ricotta
4 tbsp natural yogurt
³/₄ cup Gruyère, grated
1 egg, lightly beaten
1 cup unsalted cashew nuts
2 tbsp chopped fresh parsley
pinch of cayenne pepper

1 Sift the flour and a pinch of salt into a bowl. Beat together the egg, yogurt, water, and oil and gradually pour onto the flour, beating all the time. Stir in the spinach purée and season with pepper and nutmeg.

2 To make the filling, heat the oil in a pan and fry the scallions until translucent. Remove with a slotted spoon and drain on paper towels. Beat together the Ricotta, yogurt, and half the Gruyère. Beat in the egg and stir in the cashews and parsley. Season with salt and cayenne.

3 Heat the oil in a skillet. Pour in 3–4 tbsp of the batter and tilt the pan so that it covers the base. Cook for 3 minutes, until bubbles appear in the center. Turn and cook the other side for 2 minutes, until lightly browned. Slide the pancake onto a warm plate, cover with foil, and keep warm while you cook the rest.

4 Spread a little filling over each pancake and fold in half and then half again, envelope style. Spoon the remaining filling into the opening. Grease an ovenproof dish and arrange the pancakes in a single layer. Sprinkle with the remaining cheese and cook in a preheated oven at 350°F for 15 minutes. Garnish and serve.

Mixed Vegetable Dim Sum

Dim sum are small Chinese packets, usually served as part
of a large mixed meal. They may be filled with any variety of fillings,
steamed or fried, and served with a dipping sauce.

Serves 4

2 scallions, chopped
1 ounce green beans, chopped
1/2 small carrot, finely chopped
1 red chili, chopped
1 ounce bean sprouts, chopped
1 ounce button mushrooms, chopped
1/4 cup unsalted cashew nuts, chopped
1 small egg, beaten
2 tbsp cornstarch
1 tsp light soy sauce
1 tsp hoisin sauce
1 tsp sesame oil
32 wonton wrappers
oil, for deep-frying
1 tbsp sesame seeds

1 Mix all of the vegetables together
in a bowl and stir in the nuts, egg,
cornstarch, soy sauce, hoisin sauce,
and sesame oil, in that order, and
mix well.

2 Lay the wonton wrappers out on a
chopping board and spoon small
quantities of the mixture into the
center of each.

3 Gather the wrapper around
the filling at the top, leaving the
top open.

4 Heat the oil for deep-frying in a
wok to 350°F or until a cube of
bread browns in 30 seconds. Fry

the wontons. in batches, for
1–2 minutes or until golden brown.
Drain on absorbent paper towels.

5 Sprinkle the sesame seeds over the
wontons. Serve with a soy or plum
dipping sauce.

COOK'S TIP

If preferred, arrange the wontons
on a heatproof plate and then
steam in a steamer for 5–7 minutes,
for a healthier cooking method.

Butter-crust Tartlets with Feta Cheese

These crisp-baked bread cases, filled with sliced tomatoes,
Feta cheese, black olives, and quail's eggs, are quick to make and taste delicious.

Serves 4
8 slices bread from a medium-cut large loaf
$^1/_2$ cup butter, melted
$4^1/_2$ ounces Feta cheese, cut into small cubes
4 cherry tomatoes, cut into wedges
8 pitted black or green olives, halved
8 quail's eggs, hard-cooked
2 tbsp olive oil
1 tbsp wine vinegar
1 tsp wholegrain mustard
pinch of superfine sugar
salt and pepper
fresh parsley sprigs, to garnish

1 Remove the crusts from the bread. Trim the bread into squares and flatten each piece with a rolling pin.

2 Brush the bread with melted butter, and then arrange them in bun or muffin pans. Press a piece of crumpled foil into each bread case to secure in place. Bake in a preheated oven at 375°F for about 10 minutes, or until crisp and browned.

3 Meanwhile, mix together the Feta cheese, tomatoes, and olives. Shell the eggs and quarter them. Mix together the olive oil, vinegar, mustard, and sugar. Season with salt and pepper.

4 Remove the bread cases from the oven and discard the foil. Leave to cool slightly.

5 Just before serving, fill the bread cases with the cheese and tomato mixture. Arrange the eggs on top and spoon over the mustard dressing. Garnish with parsley sprigs and serve immediately.

COOK'S TIP

Feta cheese is made from sheep or goat's milk. It is curdled naturally without the addition of rennet.

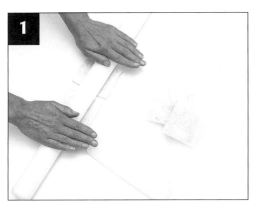

Vegetable Crêpes

Crêpes or pancakes are ideal for filling with your favorite ingredients. In this recipe
they are packed with a spicy vegetable filling which may be made in advance
and heated through for serving.

Serves 4
PANCAKES
3$^1/_2$ ounces all-purpose flour
pinch of salt
1 egg, beaten
1$^1/_4$ cups milk
vegetable oil, for frying
FILLING
2 tbsp vegetable oil
1 leek, shredded
$^1/_2$ tsp chili powder
$^1/_2$ tsp ground cumin
1$^3/_4$ ounces snow peas
3$^1/_2$ ounces button mushrooms
1 red bell pepper, sliced
$^1/_4$ cup cashew nuts, chopped
SAUCE
2 tbsp vegetarian margarine
3 tbsp all-purpose flour
$^2/_3$ cup vegetable stock
$^2/_3$ cup milk
1 tsp Dijon mustard
2$^3/_4$ ounces Cheddar cheese, grated
2 tbsp chopped cilantro

1 For the pancakes, sieve the flour
and salt into a bowl and make a well
in the center. Beat in the egg and milk
to make a batter. For the filling, heat
the oil in a skillet and sauté the leek
for 2–3 minutes. Add the rest of the
ingredients and cook for 5 minutes,
stirring. To make the sauce, melt the
margarine in a pan and add the flour.
Cook for 1 minute and remove from
the heat. Stir in the stock and milk
and return to the heat. Bring to a boil,
stirring until thick. Add the mustard,
half of the cheese, and the cilantro;
cook for 1 minute.

2 Heat 1 tbsp of oil in a non-stick 6 inch
skillet. Pour the oil from the skillet and
add an eighth of the batter, swirling it
around the base of the skillet to cover.
Cook for 2 minutes until cooked
through, turn the pancake and cook on
the other side for 1 minute. Repeat with
the remaining batter. Spoon a little of
the filling along the center of each
pancake and roll into a cigar shape. Place
in a heatproof dish and pour the sauce
over the top. Top with the remaining
cheese and heat under a hot broiler for
3–5 minutes or until the cheese melts
and turns golden.

Crisp-Fried Vegetables with Hot & Sweet Dipping Sauce

A Thai-style dipping sauce makes the perfect accompaniment
to fresh vegetables coated in a light batter and deep-fried.

Serves 4

vegetable oil, for deep-frying

1 pound 2 ounces selection of vegetables,
such as cauliflower, broccoli,
mushrooms, zucchini, bell peppers, and
baby corn cobs, cut into even-sized pieces

BATTER

1 cup all-purpose flour

$1/2$ tsp salt

1 tsp superfine sugar

1 tsp baking powder

3 tbsp vegetable oil

scant 1 cup warm water

SAUCE

6 tbsp light malt vinegar

2 tbsp Thai fish sauce or
light soy sauce

2 tbsp water

1 tbsp soft brown sugar

salt

2 garlic cloves, crushed

2 tsp grated ginger root

2 red chilies, seeded and
chopped finely

2 tbsp chopped fresh cilantro

1 To make the batter, sift the flour,
salt, sugar, and baking powder into a
large bowl. Add the oil and most of
the water. Whisk together to make a
smooth batter, adding extra water to
give it the consistency of light cream.
Chill for 20–30 minutes.

2 Meanwhile, make the sauce. Heat the
vinegar, fish sauce or soy sauce, water,
sugar, and a pinch of salt until boiling.
Remove from the heat and leave to cool.

3 Mix together the garlic, ginger,
chilies, and cilantro in a small serving
bowl. Add the cooled vinegar mixture
and stir together.

4 Heat the vegetable oil for deep-
frying in a wok or deep-fryer. Dip the
prepared vegetables in the batter and
fry them, a few at a time, until crisp
and golden—about 2 minutes. Drain
on paper towels.

5 Serve the vegetables accompanied
by the dipping sauce.

Watercress & Cheese Tartlets

These individual tartlets are great for lunchtime or for picnic food. Watercress is a good source of folic acid, which is important in early pregnancy.

Makes 4
³/₄ cup all-purpose flour
salt
¹/₂ cup butter or vegetarian margarine
2–3 tbsp cold water
2 bunches watercress
2 garlic cloves, crushed
1 shallot, chopped
5¹/₂ ounces Cheddar cheese, grated
4 tbsp natural yogurt
¹/₂ tsp paprika

1 Sieve the flour into a bowl and add a pinch of salt. Rub 1³/₄ ounces of the butter or margarine into the flour until the mixture resembles bread crumbs. Stir in the cold water to make a dough.

2 Roll the dough out on a floured surface and use to line four 4 inch tartlet pans. Prick the bases with a fork and leave to chill in the refrigerator.

3 Heat the remaining butter or margarine in a skillet. Discard the stems from the watercress and add to the skillet together with the garlic and shallot, cooking for 1–2 minutes until the watercress is wilted. Remove the pan from the heat and stir in the cheese, yogurt, and paprika. Spoon the mixture into the pastry cases and cook in a preheated oven at 350°F for 20 minutes or until the filling is firm. Turn out the tartlets and serve.

VARIATION

Use spinach instead of the watercress, making sure it is well drained before mixing with the remaining filling ingredients.

Vegetable Enchiladas

This Mexican dish uses prepared tortillas which are readily available in supermarkets.
They are filled with a spicy vegetable mixture and topped with a hot tomato sauce.

Serves 4
4 flour tortillas
$^3/_4$ cup Cheddar, grated

FILLING

$2^3/_4$ ounces spinach
2 tbsp olive oil
8 baby corn cobs, sliced
1 tbsp frozen peas, thawed
1 red bell pepper, diced
1 carrot, diced
1 leek, sliced
2 garlic cloves, crushed
1 red chili, chopped
salt and pepper

SAUCE

$1^1/_4$ cups sieved tomatoes
2 shallots, chopped
1 garlic clove, crushed
$1^1/_4$ cups vegetable stock
1 tsp superfine sugar
1 tsp chili powder

1 To make the filling, blanch the spinach in a pan of boiling water for 2 minutes, drain well, and chop.

2 Heat the oil in a skillet and sauté the corn, peas, bell pepper, carrot, leek, garlic, and chili for 3–4 minutes. Stir in the spinach and season with salt and pepper to taste.

3 Put all of the sauce ingredients in a saucepan and bring to a boil, stirring to combine. Cook over a high heat for 20 minutes, stirring occasionally, until thickened and reduced by about a third.

4 Spoon a quarter of the filling along the center of each tortilla.

5 Roll the tortillas around the filling and place in an ovenproof dish, seam-side down.

6 Pour the sauce over the tortillas and sprinkle the cheese on top. Cook in a preheated oven at 350°F for 20 minutes or until the cheese has melted and browned. Serve immediately.

Mediterranean Vegetable Tart

A rich tomato pastry base topped with a mouth-watering selection of vegetables
and cheese makes a dish that's tasty as well as attractive.

Serves 6
1 eggplant, sliced
2 tbsp salt
4 tbsp olive oil
1 garlic clove, crushed
1 large yellow bell pepper, seeded and sliced
1¼ cups ready-made tomato pasta sauce
⅔ cup sun-dried tomatoes in oil, drained and halved if necessary
6 ounces Mozzarella, drained and sliced thinly

PASTRY

2 cups all-purpose flour
pinch of celery salt
½ cup butter or vegetarian margarine
2 tbsp tomato paste
2–3 tbsp milk

1 To make the pastry, sift the flour and celery salt into a bowl. Rub in the butter or margarine until the mixture resembles fine bread crumbs. Mix the tomato paste and milk and stir into the mixture to form a firm dough. Knead on a floured surface until smooth. Wrap and chill for 30 minutes.

2 Grease a 11 inch loose-bottomed flan pan. Roll out the pastry on a floured surface and use to line the pan. Trim and prick all over with a fork. Chill for 30 minutes.

3 Layer the eggplant in a dish, sprinkling with the salt. Leave for 30 minutes.

4 Bake the pastry case in a preheated oven at 400°F for 20–25 minutes until cooked and golden. Remove from the oven and set aside. Increase the oven temperature to 450°F.

5 Rinse the eggplant and pat dry with paper towels. Heat three tablespoons of the oil in a skillet and fry the garlic, eggplant, and bell pepper for 5–6 minutes until softened. Drain well. Spread the pasta sauce over the pastry case and arrange the cooked vegetables, sundried tomatoes, and Mozzarella on top. Brush with oil and bake for 5 minutes until the cheese is just melting. Serve immediately.

Cheese & Garlic Mushroom Pizza

This pizza dough is flavored with garlic and herbs and topped with
mixed mushrooms and melting cheese for a really delicious pizza.

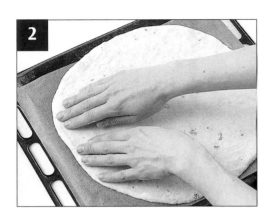

Serves 4
DOUGH
3½ cups strong white flour
2 tsp easy-blend yeast
2 garlic cloves, crushed
2 tbsp chopped thyme
2 tbsp olive oil
1¼ cups tepid water
TOPPING
2 tbsp butter or vegetarian margarine
12 ounces mixed mushrooms, sliced
2 garlic cloves, crushed
2 tbsp chopped parsley
2 tbsp tomato paste
6 tbsp sieved tomatoes
2¾ ounces Mozzarella cheese, grated
salt and pepper
chopped parsley, to garnish

1 Put the flour, yeast, garlic, and
thyme in a mixing bowl. Make a well
in the center and gradually stir in the
oil and water. Bring together to form a
soft dough.

2 Turn the dough onto a floured
surface and knead for 5 minutes or
until smooth. Roll into a 14 inch
round and place on a greased cookie

COOK'S TIP

If preferred, spread the base with a
prepared cheese sauce before
adding the mushrooms.

sheet. Leave in a warm place for 20
minutes or until the dough puffs up.

3 Meanwhile, make the topping. Melt
the margarine or butter in a skillet and
sauté the mushrooms, garlic, and
parsley for 5 minutes. Mix the tomato
paste and sieved tomatoes and spoon
onto the pizza base, leaving a ½ inch
edge of dough. Spoon the mushroom
mixture on top. Season with salt and
pepper to taste and sprinkle the
cheese on top. Cook the pizza in a
preheated oven at 375°F for 20–25
minutes or until the base is crisp and
the cheese has melted. Garnish with
chopped parsley and serve
immediately.

Fried Bean Curd with Peanut Sauce

This is a very sociable dish if put in the center of the table where people can help themselves with toothpicks.

Serves 4
1 pound 2 ounces marinated or plain bean curd
4 cups sunflower oil
2 tbsp sesame oil
BATTER
4 tbsp all-purpose flour
2 eggs, beaten
4 tbsp milk
½ tsp baking powder
½ tsp chili powder
PEANUT SAUCE
2 tbsp rice vinegar
2 tbsp sugar
1 tsp salt
3 tbsp smooth peanut butter
½ tsp chili flakes
3 tbsp barbecue sauce

1 Cut the bean curd into 1 inch triangles. Set aside until required.

2 To make the sauce, combine the vinegar, sugar, and salt in a saucepan. Bring to a boil and then simmer for 2 minutes. Remove from the heat and add the peanut butter, chili flakes, and barbecue sauce, stirring to mix.

3 To make the batter, sift the flour into a bowl. Make a well in the center and add the eggs. Using a metal spoon, draw in the flour, adding the milk slowly. Add the baking powder and chili powder, stirring to form a batter.

4 Heat the oils in a deep-fryer or large wok until a light haze appears on top. Dip the bean curd triangles into the batter and deep-fry until golden. Drain and serve with the sauce.

COOK'S TIP

Bean curd is rich in protein, iron, calcium, and B vitamins.

Baked Eggplant, Basil, & Mozzarella Rolls

Thin slices of eggplant are fried in olive oil and garlic,
and then topped with pesto sauce and finely sliced Mozzarella.

Serves 4
2 eggplants, sliced thinly lengthwise
5 tbsp olive oil
1 garlic clove, crushed
4 tbsp pesto
1½ cups Mozzarella, grated
basil leaves, torn into pieces
salt and pepper
fresh basil leaves, to garnish

1 Sprinkle the eggplant slices liberally with salt and leave for 10–15 minutes to extract the bitter juices. Turn the slices over and repeat on the other side. Rinse well with cold water and drain thoroughly on paper towels.

2 Heat the olive oil in a large skillet and add the garlic. Add the eggplant slices, in batches, and fry lightly on both sides. Drain well on paper towels.

3 Spread the pesto onto one side of the eggplant slices.

4 Top with the grated Mozzarella and sprinkle with the torn basil leaves. Season with a little salt and pepper to taste.

5 Roll up the slices and secure with wooden toothpicks.

6 Arrange the eggplant rolls in a greased ovenproof baking dish and cook in a preheated oven at 350°F for about 8–10 minutes.

7 Transfer the baked eggplant, basil, and Mozzarella rolls to a warmed serving plate.

8 Scatter with fresh basil leaves and serve at once.

COOK'S TIP

You may find it easier to slice the Mozzarella rather than grate it yourself.

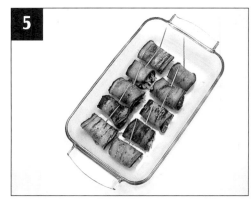

Barbecue Bean Burgers

These tasty burgers are ideal for a barbecue in the summer but they are equally delicious cooked indoors at any time of year.

Serves 6
1/3 cup aduki beans
1/3 cup black-eye peas
6 tbsp vegetable oil
1 large onion, chopped finely
1 tsp yeast extract
4 1/2 ounces grated carrot
1 1/2 cups fresh whole wheat bread crumbs
2 tbsp whole wheat flour
salt and pepper
BARBECUE SAUCE
1/3 tsp chili powder
1 tsp celery salt
2 tbsp light muscovado sugar
2 tbsp red wine vinegar
2 tbsp vegetarian Worcestershire sauce
3 tbsp tomato paste
dash of Tabasco sauce
TO SERVE
6 whole wheat baps, toasted
mixed green salad
jacket potato fries

1 Place the beans in separate saucepans, cover with water, and bring to a boil. Cover and simmer the aduki beans for 40 minutes and the black-eye peas for 50 minutes, or until tender. Drain and rinse well.

2 Transfer to a mixing bowl and lightly mash together with a potato masher or fork. Set aside.

3 Heat 1 tablespoon of the oil in a skillet and gently fry the onion for 3–4 minutes until softened. Mix into the beans with the yeast extract, grated carrot, bread crumbs, and seasoning. Bind together well.

4 With wet hands, divide the mixture into 6 and form into burgers 3 1/2 inches in diameter. Put the flour on a plate and use to coat the burgers.

5 Heat the remaining oil in a large skillet and cook the burgers for 3–4 minutes on each side, turning carefully, until golden and crisp. Drain on paper towels.

6 Meanwhile, make the sauce. Mix all the ingredients together until well blended. Place the burgers in the toasted baps and serve with a mixed green salad, jacket potato fries, and a spoonful of the barbecue sauce.

Corn-on-the-cob

Corn-on-the-cob is available nearly all the year round,
and it can be barbecued with the husk on or off.

Serves 4-6
4–6 corn-on-the-cobs
oil, for brushing
TO SERVE
butter (optional)
salt (optional)

1 Soak the corn cobs in hand-hot water for 20 minutes. Drain thoroughly.

2 If the corn cobs have no husks, brush generously with oil and cook over a hot barbecue for 30 minutes, brushing occasionally with the oil and turning often.

3 If your corn cobs have husks, tear off all but the last two layers and brush with oil.

4 Cook over a hot barbecue for 40 minutes, brushing with oil once or twice, and turning occasionally.

5 Serve hot, without the husks. Add a knob of butter and salt to taste

COOK'S TIP

Try to buy the corn cobs with the husk still on, as they will retain more moisture this way. While you are barbecuing the corn cobs, you may like to flavor them with herbs —try tucking some fresh rosemary, cilantro, or thyme inside the husk for an aromatic flavor.

Bean Curd & Mushroom Brochettes

These bean curd and mushroom brochettes are marinated in a lemon,
garlic, and herb mixture so that they soak up a delicious flavor.

Serves 4
1 lemon
1 garlic clove, crushed
4 tbsp olive oil
4 tbsp white wine vinegar
1 tbsp chopped fresh herbs, such as rosemary, parsley, and thyme
10½ ounces smoked bean curd
12 ounces mushrooms, wiped
salt and pepper
fresh herbs, to garnish
TO SERVE
mixed salad greens
cherry tomatoes, halved

1 Grate the rind from the lemon finely and squeeze out the juice.

2 Add the garlic, olive oil, vinegar, and herbs to the lemon rind and juice, mixing well. Season with salt and pepper to taste.

3 Slice the bean curd into large chunks. Thread the bean curd onto metal or wooden skewers, alternating the bean curd with the mushrooms.

4 Lay the kabobs in a shallow dish and pour over the marinade. Cover and chill in the refrigerator for 1–2 hours, turning the kabobs in the marinade from time to time.

5 Cook the kabobs over a hot barbecue, brushing them with the marinade, and turning often, for about 6 minutes.

6 Garnish with fresh herbs and serve with mixed salad greens and cherry tomatoes.

COOK'S TIP

Soak wooden skewers in hand–hot water for 30 minutes to prevent them from burning during cooking.

Nan Bread with Curried Vegetable Kabobs

Warmed Indian bread is served with barbecued vegetable kabobs, which are brushed with a curry-spiced yogurt baste.

Serves 4

nan bread, to serve

sprigs of fresh mint, to garnish

YOGURT BASTE

$2/3$ cup natural yogurt

1 tbsp chopped fresh mint
or 1 tsp dried mint

1 tsp ground cumin

1 tsp ground coriander

$1/2$ tsp chili powder

pinch of turmeric

pinch of ground ginger

salt and pepper

KABOBS

8 small new potatoes

1 small eggplant

1 zucchini, cut into chunks

8 crimini or closed-
cap mushrooms

8 small tomatoes

1 To make the spiced yogurt baste, mix together the yogurt, mint, cumin, coriander, chili powder, turmeric, and ginger. Season with salt and pepper, cover, and chill.

2 Cook the potatoes in a saucepan of boiling water until just tender. Chop the eggplant into chunks and sprinkle them liberally with salt. Leave for 10–15 minutes to extract the bitter juices. Rinse and drain them well. Drain the potatoes.

3 If using wooden skewers, soak them in warm water for 30 minutes. Thread all of the vegetables onto 4 metal or wooden skewers, alternating the different types of vegetables.

4 Place the kabobs in a shallow dish and brush with the yogurt baste, coating them evenly. Cover and chill until ready to cook.

5 Wrap the nan bread in foil and place towards one side of the barbecue to warm through.

6 Cook the kabobs over the barbecue, basting with any remaining spiced yogurt, until they just begin to char slightly. Serve with the warmed nan bread, garnished with sprigs of fresh mint.

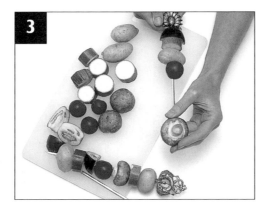

Pasta Dishes

Pasta is one of the most popular and versatile foods on sale today. Available fresh or dried, pasta is made in a wide variety of colors and flavors, shapes and sizes, each lending itself to a particular type of sauce. For instance, flat ribbons go well with cream or cheese-based sauces, while tubes and shapes are ideal for trapping chunkier sauces in their crevices.

Whole wheat pastas have a chewier texture and are valuable for the additional fiber they contain. Pasta is a

marvelous convenience food—it is both nourishing and satisfying. All types of pasta are quick to cook and provide good basic food that can be dressed up in all kinds of ways. Pasta combines very well with vegetables, herbs, nuts, and cheeses, to provide scores of interesting and tasty vegetarian meals.

Spinach Gnocchi with Tomato & Basil Sauce

These gnocchi or small dumplings are made with potato and flavored with spinach and nutmeg and served in a rich tomato sauce for an ideal light meal.

Serves 4
1 pound baking potatoes
2³/₄ ounces spinach
1 tsp water
3 tbsp butter or vegetarian margarine
1 small egg, beaten
³/₄ cup all-purpose flour
fresh basil sprigs, to garnish

TOMATO SAUCE
1 tbsp olive oil
1 shallot, chopped
1 tbsp tomato paste
8 ounce can chopped tomatoes
2 tbsp chopped basil
6 tbsp red wine
1 tsp superfine sugar
salt and pepper

1 To make the gnocchi, cook the potatoes in their skins in a pan of boiling, salted water for 20 minutes or until cooked through. Drain well and press through a sieve, using the back of a spoon, into a bowl.

2 Meanwhile, cook the spinach in 1 tsp water for 5 minutes until wilted. Drain and pat dry with paper towels. Chop and stir into the potatoes.

3 Add the butter or vegetarian margarine, egg, and half of the flour to the potato mixture, mixing well. Turn out onto a floured surface, gradually kneading in the remaining flour to form a soft dough. With floured hands, roll the dough into thin ropes and cut off ³/₄ inch pieces. Press the center of each dumpling with your finger, drawing it towards you to curl the sides of the gnocchi. Cover and leave to chill in the refrigerator.

4 Heat the oil for the sauce in a pan and sauté the shallots for 5 minutes. Add the tomato paste, tomatoes, basil, red wine, and sugar and season well.

Bring to a boil and then simmer for 20 minutes.

5 Bring a pan of salted water to a boil and cook the gnocchi for 2–3 minutes or until they rise to the top of the pan. Drain well and transfer to serving dishes. Spoon the tomato sauce over the top. Garnish and serve.

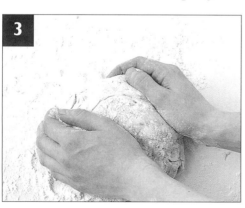

Vegetable Pasta Nests

These large pasta nests look impressive when presented filled
with broiled mixed vegetables, and taste delicious.

Serves 4
6 ounces spaghetti
1 eggplant, halved and sliced
1 zucchini, diced
1 red bell pepper, seeded and chopped diagonally
6 tbsp olive oil
2 garlic cloves, crushed
4 tbsp butter or vegetarian margarine, melted
1 tbsp dry white bread crumbs
salt and pepper
fresh parsley sprigs, to garnish

1 Bring a large saucepan of water
to a boil and cook the spaghetti until
"al dente", or according to the
instructions on the packet. Drain.

2 Place the eggplant, zucchini, and
bell pepper on a cookie sheet.

3 Mix the oil and garlic together and
pour over the vegetables, tossing
to coat.

4 Cook under a preheated hot broiler
for about 10 minutes, turning, until
tender and lightly charred. Set aside
and keep warm.

5 Divide the spaghetti among 4
lightly greased Yorkshire pudding
pans. Using a fork, curl the spaghetti
to form nests.

6 Brush the pasta nests with melted
butter or vegetarian margarine and
sprinkle with the bread crumbs. Bake
in a preheated oven at 400°F for

15 minutes or until lightly golden.
Remove the pasta nests from the pans
and transfer to serving plates. Divide
the broiled vegetables between the
pasta nests, season, and garnish with
fresh parsley.

COOK'S TIP

"Al dente" means "to the bite" and
describes cooked pasta that is not
too soft, but still has a bite to it.

Spring Vegetable & Bean Curd Fusilli

This is a simple, clean-tasting dish of green vegetables,
bean curd, and pasta, lightly tossed in olive oil.

Serves 4
9 ounces asparagus
4$\frac{1}{2}$ ounces snow peas
9 ounces green beans
1 leek
9 ounces shelled small fava beans
10$\frac{1}{2}$ ounces dried fusilli
2 tbsp olive oil
2 tbsp butter or vegetarian margarine
1 garlic clove, crushed
9 ounces bean curd, cut into 1 inch cubes
$\frac{1}{3}$ cup pitted green olives in brine, drained
salt and pepper
freshly grated Parmesan, to serve

1 Using a sharp knife, cut the asparagus into 2 inch lengths. Finely slice the snow peas diagonally and slice the green beans into 1 inch pieces. Finely slice the leek.

2 Bring a large saucepan of water to a boil and add the asparagus, green beans, and fava beans. Bring back to a boil and cook for 4 minutes until just tender. Drain well and rinse in cold water. Set aside.

3 Bring a large pan of salted water to a boil and cook the fusilli for 8–9 minutes until just tender. Drain well. Toss in 1 tbsp of the oil and season to taste.

4 Meanwhile, in a wok or large skillet, heat the remaining oil and the butter or margarine and gently fry the

leek, garlic, and bean curd for 1–2 minutes until the vegetables have just softened.

5 Stir in the snow peas and cook for another minute.

6 Add the boiled vegetables and olives to the pan and heat through for 1 minute. Carefully stir in the pasta and seasoning. Cook for 1 minute and pile into a warmed serving dish. Serve sprinkled with Parmesan.

Fried Noodles with Bean Sprouts, Chives, & Chilies

This is a simple idea to jazz up noodles which accompany
main course dishes in Thailand.

Serves 4
1 pound 2 ounces medium egg noodles
1 cup bean sprouts
$\frac{1}{2}$ ounce chives
3 tbsp sunflower oil
1 garlic clove, crushed
4 green chilies, deseeded, sliced, and soaked in
2 tbsp rice vinegar
salt

1 To cook the noodles, soak them in boiling water for 10 minutes. Drain and set aside.

2 Soak the bean sprouts in cold water while you cut the chives into 1 inch pieces. Set a few chives aside for garnish. Drain the bean sprouts thoroughly.

3 Heat the oil in a wok or large, heavy skillet. Add the crushed garlic and stir; then add the chilies and stir until fragrant, about 1 minute.

4 Add the bean sprouts, stir, and then add the noodles. Stir in a little salt and the chives. Using 2 spoons, lift and stir the noodles for 1 minute.

5 Garnish the finished dish with the reserved chives, and serve immediately.

Vegetable-filled Ravioli

These small packets are very easy to make and have
the advantage of being filled with your favorite mixture of succulent mushrooms.
Serve with freshly grated cheese sprinkled on top.

Serves 4
FILLING
3 tbsp butter or
vegetarian margarine
2 garlic cloves, crushed
1 small leek, chopped
2 celery sticks, chopped
2$^1/_3$ cups open-cap mushrooms,
chopped
1 egg, beaten
2 tbsp grated Parmesan cheese
salt and pepper
RAVIOLI
4 sheets filo pastry
3 tbsp vegetarian margarine
oil, for deep-frying

1 To make the filling, melt the butter or margarine in a skillet and sauté the garlic and leek for 2–3 minutes. Add the celery and mushrooms and cook for a further 4–5 minutes until all of the vegetables are tender.

2 Turn off the heat and stir in the egg and Parmesan cheese. Season with salt and pepper to taste.

3 Lay the pastry sheets on a chopping board and cut each into nine squares. Spoon a little of the filling into the center half of the squares and brush the edges of the pastry with butter or margarine. Lay another square on top and seal the edges to make a packet.

4 Heat the oil for deep-frying to 350°F or until a cube of bread browns in 30 seconds. Fry the ravioli, in batches, for 2–3 minutes or until golden brown. Remove from the oil with a slotted spoon and pat dry on absorbent paper towels. Transfer to a warm serving plate and serve.

COOK'S TIP

If time is short, boil some frozen mixed vegetables and use as a quick filling for the ravioli.

Pasta with Pine Nuts & Blue Cheese

Simple, quick, and inexpensive, this tasty pasta dish
can be prepared in minutes.

Serves 4
1 cup pine nuts
12 ounces dried pasta shapes
2 zucchini, sliced
4¹/₂ ounces broccoli, broken into florets
1 cup full-fat soft cheese
²/₃ cup milk
1 tbsp chopped fresh basil
4¹/₂ ounces button mushrooms, sliced
3 ounces blue cheese, crumbled
salt and pepper
sprigs of fresh basil, to garnish
green salad, to serve

1 Scatter the pine nuts onto a cookie
sheet and cook under a preheated
broiler, turning occasionally, until
lightly browned all over. Be careful
not to burn them as they broil very
quickly. Set aside.

2 Cook the pasta in a pan of boiling,
salted water for about 8–10 minutes
until just tender. Meanwhile, cook
the zucchini and broccoli in a small
amount of boiling, lightly salted
water for 5 minutes or until tender.

3 Put the soft cheese into a saucepan
and heat gently, stirring constantly.
Add the milk and stir to mix.

4 Add the basil and mushrooms and
cook gently for 2–3 minutes. Stir in
the blue cheese and season.

5 Drain the pasta and the vegetables
and mix together. Pour the cheese
and mushroom sauce over and add
the pine nuts. Toss gently to mix.
Garnish with basil sprigs and serve
with a green salad.

COOK'S TIP

Watch the pine nuts carefully,
otherwise they will burn. They will
toast in 2–3 minutes.

Vegetable Lasagne

This colorful and tasty lasagne, with layers of vegetables in tomato sauce and eggplants, all topped with a rich cheese sauce, is simply delicious.

Serves 4
1 eggplant, sliced
3 tbsp olive oil
2 garlic cloves, crushed
1 red onion, halved and sliced
1 green bell pepper, diced
1 red bell pepper, diced
1 yellow bell pepper, diced
8 ounces mixed mushrooms, sliced
2 celery sticks, sliced
1 zucchini, diced
$^{1}/_{2}$ tsp chili powder
$^{1}/_{2}$ tsp ground cumin
2 tomatoes, chopped
$1^{1}/_{4}$ cups sieved tomatoes
2 tbsp chopped basil
8 no pre-cook lasagne verdi sheets

CHEESE SAUCE

2 tbsp butter or vegetarian margarine
1 tbsp flour
$^{2}/_{3}$ cup vegetable stock
$1^{1}/_{4}$ cups milk
$^{3}/_{4}$ cup Cheddar, grated
1 tsp Dijon mustard
1 tbsp chopped basil
1 egg, beaten

1 Place the eggplant slices in a colander, sprinkle with salt, and leave for 20 minutes. Rinse under cold water, drain, and reserve. Heat the oil in a pan and sauté the garlic and onion for 1–2 minutes. Add the bell peppers, mushrooms, celery, and zucchini and cook for 3–4 minutes, stirring. Stir in the spices and cook for 1 minute. Mix the tomatoes, sieved tomatoes, and basil together and season well.

2 For the sauce, melt the butter in a pan, add the flour, and cook for 1 minute. Remove from the heat and stir in the stock and milk. Return to the heat and add half of the cheese and the mustard. Boil, stirring, until thickened. Stir in the basil and season. Remove the pan from the heat and stir in the egg. Place half of the lasagne sheets in an ovenproof dish. Top with half of the vegetables, then half of the tomato sauce. Cover with half the eggplants. Repeat and spoon the cheese sauce on top. Sprinkle with cheese and cook in a preheated oven at 350°F for 40 minutes.

Pasta Provençale

A Mediterranean mixture of red bell peppers, garlic, and zucchini,
cooked in olive oil and tossed with pasta.

Serves 4
3 tbsp olive oil
1 onion, sliced
2 garlic cloves, chopped
3 red bell peppers, deseeded and cut into strips
3 zucchini, sliced
14 ounce can chopped tomatoes
3 tbsp sun-dried tomato paste
2 tbsp chopped fresh basil
9 ounces fresh pasta spirals
1 cup grated Gruyère cheese
salt and pepper
fresh basil sprigs to garnish

1 Heat the oil in a heavy-based saucepan or flameproof casserole.

2 Add the onion and garlic and cook for 3–4 minutes, stirring occasionally, until softened.

3 Add the bell peppers and zucchini and fry for 5 minutes, stirring occasionally.

4 Add the tomatoes, sun-dried tomato paste, basil, and salt and pepper to taste, cover, and cook for 5 minutes, stirring.

5 Meanwhile, bring a large saucepan of salted water to a boil and add the pasta. Stir and bring back to a boil. Reduce the heat slightly and cook, uncovered, for 3 minutes, or until just tender. Drain the pasta thoroughly in a colander.

6 Add the pasta to the vegetables and toss gently to mix well. Put the mixture into a shallow ovenproof dish and sprinkle with the cheese.

7 Cook under a preheated broiler for 5 minutes until the cheese is golden brown. Garnish with fresh basil sprigs and serve.

Tagliatelle Tricolore with Broccoli & Cheese Sauce

Some of the simplest and most satisfying dishes are made with pasta, such as this delicious combination of tagliatelle with its two-cheese sauce.

Serves 4
10$\frac{1}{2}$ ounces dried tagliatelle tricolore (plain, spinach- and tomato-flavored noodles)
9 ounces broccoli, broken into small flowerets
1$\frac{1}{2}$ cups Mascarpone cheese
1 cup blue cheese, chopped
1 tbsp chopped fresh oregano
2 tbsp butter
salt and pepper
sprigs of fresh oregano, to garnish
freshly grated Parmesan, to serve

1 Cook the tagliatelle in a saucepan of boiling, salted water until just tender, according to the instructions on the packet.

2 Meanwhile, cook the broccoli flowerets in a small amount of lightly salted, boiling water. Avoid overcooking the broccoli, so that it retains its color and texture.

3 Heat the Mascarpone and blue cheeses together gently in a large saucepan until they are melted.

4 Stir in the oregano and season with salt and pepper to taste.

5 Drain the tagliatelle thoroughly and return to the pan. Add the cheese sauce and butter and toss to coat.

6 Drain the broccoli and add to the pasta, tossing to mix.

7 Divide the pasta between 4 warmed serving plates.

8 Garnish with sprigs of fresh oregano and serve with freshly grated Parmesan cheese.

COOK'S TIP

Choose your favorite pasta shapes as an alternative to tagliatelle, if you prefer.

Vegetable Cannelloni

This dish is made with prepared cannelloni tubes,
but may also be made by rolling ready-bought lasagne sheets.

Serves 4
1 eggplant
$^1/_2$ cup olive oil
8 ounces spinach
2 garlic cloves, crushed
1 tsp ground cumin
1 cup mushrooms, chopped
12 cannelloni tubes
salt and pepper

TOMATO SAUCE
1 tbsp olive oil
1 onion, chopped
2 garlic cloves, crushed
2 x 14 ounce cans chopped tomatoes
1 tsp superfine sugar
2 tbsp chopped basil
$1^3/_4$ ounces Mozzarella, sliced

1 Cut the eggplant into small dice.

2 Heat the oil in a skillet and cook the eggplant for 2–3 minutes.

3 Add the spinach, garlic, cumin, and mushrooms. Season to taste and cook for 2–3 minutes, stirring. Spoon the mixture into the cannelloni tubes and place in an ovenproof dish in a single layer.

4 To make the sauce, heat the olive oil in a saucepan and sauté the onion and garlic for 1 minute. Add the tomatoes, superfine sugar, and basil and bring to a boil. Reduce the heat and simmer for 5 minutes. Pour the sauce over the cannelloni tubes.

5 Arrange the sliced Mozzarella on top of the sauce and cook in a preheated oven at 375°F for 30 minutes or until the cheese is bubbling and golden brown. Serve immediately.

COOK'S TIP

You can prepare the tomato sauce in advance and store it in the refrigerator for up to 24 hours.

Three-Cheese Macaroni Bake

Based on a traditional family favorite, this pasta bake has plenty of flavor.
Serve with a crisp salad for a quick, tasty supper.

Serves 4
2¹/₂ cups Béchamel Sauce (see page 14)
2 cups macaroni
1 egg, beaten
1 cup grated sharp Cheddar
1 tbsp wholegrain mustard
2 tbsp chopped fresh chives
4 tomatoes, sliced
1 cup grated brick cheese
¹/₂ cup grated blue cheese
2 tbsp sunflower seeds
salt and pepper
snipped fresh chives, to garnish

1 Make the béchamel sauce, put into a bowl and cover with plastic wrap to prevent a skin forming. Set aside until required.

2 Bring a saucepan of salted water to a boil and cook the macaroni for 8–10 minutes until just tender. Drain well and place in an ovenproof dish.

3 Stir the beaten egg, Cheddar, mustard, chives, and salt and pepper to taste into the béchamel sauce. Spoon the sauce over the macaroni, making sure it is well covered.

4 Arrange a layer of sliced tomatoes on top of the sauce.

5 Sprinkle over the brick and blue cheeses, and the sunflower seeds.

6 Place on a cookie sheet and bake in a preheated oven at 375°F for 25–30 minutes until bubbling and golden.

7 Garnish the macaroni bake with freshly snipped chives and serve immediately.

Tagliatelle with Zucchini Sauce

This is a really fresh tasting dish which is ideal with
a crisp white wine and some crusty bread.

Serves 4
1 pound 7 ounces zucchini
6 tbsp olive oil
3 garlic cloves, crushed
3 tbsp chopped basil
2 red chilies, sliced
juice of 1 large lemon
5 tbsp light cream
4 tbsp grated Parmesan cheese
8 ounces tagliatelle
salt and pepper

1 Using a vegetable peeler, slice the zucchini into thin ribbons.

2 Heat the oil in a skillet and sauté the garlic for 30 seconds. Add the zucchini and cook over a gentle heat, stirring, for 5–7 minutes.

3 Stir in the basil, chilies, lemon juice, cream, and Parmesan and season with salt and pepper to taste.

4 Meanwhile, cook the pasta in a large pan of boiling salted water for 10 minutes until "al dente". Drain well and put in a warm serving bowl. Pile the zucchini mixture on top of the pasta. Serve immediately.

COOK'S VARIATION

Lime juice and zest could be
used instead of the lemon
as an alternative.

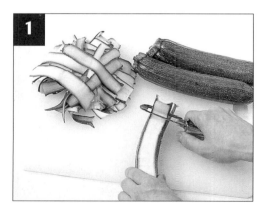

Spaghetti with Pear & Walnut Sauce

This is quite an unusual combination of ingredients in a savory dish, but is absolutely wonderful tossed into a fine pasta such as spaghetti.

Serves 4
8 ounces spaghetti
2 small ripe pears, peeled and sliced
$^2/_3$ cup vegetable stock
6 tbsp dry white wine
2 tbsp butter
1 tbsp olive oil
1 red onion, quartered and sliced
1 garlic clove, crushed
$^1/_2$ cup walnut halves
2 tbsp chopped oregano
1 tbsp lemon juice
$^3/_4$ cup Dolcelatte cheese
salt and pepper
fresh oregano sprigs, to garnish

1 Cook the pasta in a saucepan of boiling, salted water for 8–10 minutes or until "al dente". Drain thoroughly.

2 Meanwhile, place the pears in a pan and pour over the stock and wine. Poach the pears over a gentle heat for 10 minutes. Drain and reserve the cooking liquid and pears.

3 Melt the butter with the oil and sauté the red onion and garlic for 2–3 minutes, stirring.

4 Add the walnuts, oregano, and lemon juice, stirring.

5 Stir in the pears and 4 tablespoons of the poaching liquid.

6 Crumble the Dolcelatte cheese into the pan and cook over a gentle heat, stirring occasionally, for 1–2 minutes or until the cheese just begins to melt.

Season the sauce with salt and pepper to taste.

7 Toss the pasta into the sauce, garnish, and serve.

COOK'S TIP

You can use any good-flavored blue cheese for this dish.

Olive, Bell Pepper, & Tomato Pasta

The sweet cherry tomatoes in this recipe add color and flavor
and are complemented by the black olives and bell peppers.

Serves 4
8 ounces penne
2 tbsp olive oil
2 tbsp butter
2 garlic cloves, crushed
1 green bell pepper, thinly sliced
1 yellow bell pepper, thinly sliced
16 cherry tomatoes, halved
1 tbsp chopped oregano
1/2 cup dry white wine
2 tbsp quartered, pitted black olives
2 3/4 ounces arugula
salt and pepper
fresh oregano sprigs, to garnish

1 Cook the pasta in a saucepan of
boiling, salted water for 8–10 minutes
or until "al dente". Drain thoroughly.

2 Heat the oil and butter in a pan
until the butter melts. Sauté the garlic
for 30 seconds. Add the bell peppers
and cook for 3–4 minutes, stirring.

3 Stir in the cherry tomatoes,
oregano, wine, and olives and cook
for 3–4 minutes. Season well and stir
in the arugula until just wilted.

4 Transfer the pasta to a serving dish
and spoon the sauce on top. Toss well
to mix, garnish, and serve.

COOK'S TIP

Ensure that the saucepan is
large enough to prevent the
pasta from sticking together
during cooking

Baked Pasta in Tomato Sauce

This pasta dish is baked in a pudding basin and cut into slices for serving.
It looks and tastes terrific and is perfect when you want to impress.

Serves 8
3¹/₂ ounces pasta shapes, such as penne or casareccia
1 tbsp olive oil
1 leek, chopped
3 garlic cloves, crushed
1 green bell pepper, chopped
14 ounce can chopped tomatoes
2 tbsp chopped, pitted black olives
2 eggs, beaten
1 tbsp chopped basil
TOMATO SAUCE
1 tbsp olive oil
1 onion, chopped
8 ounce can chopped tomatoes
1 tsp superfine sugar
2 tbsp tomato paste
²/₃ cup vegetable stock
salt and pepper

1 Cook the pasta in a saucepan of boiling, salted water for 8 minutes. Drain thoroughly.

2 Meanwhile, heat the oil in a saucepan and sauté the leek and garlic for 2 minutes, stirring. Add the bell pepper, tomatoes, and olives and cook for a further 5 minutes.

3 Remove the pan from the heat and stir in the pasta, beaten eggs, and basil. Season well and spoon into a lightly greased 2 pint ovenproof pudding basin.

4 Place the pudding basin in a roasting pan and half-fill the pan with boiling water. Cover and cook in a preheated oven at 350°F for 40 minutes until set.

5 To make the sauce, heat the oil in a pan and sauté the onion for 2 minutes. Add the remaining ingredients and cook for 10 minutes. Put the sauce in a food processor or blender and blend until smooth. Return to a clean saucepan and heat until hot.

6 Turn the pasta out of the pudding basin onto a warm plate. Slice and serve with the tomato sauce.

Thai-Style Noodles

This dish is considered the Thai national dish, as it is made and eaten everywhere—a one-dish fast food for eating on the move.

Serves 4
9 ounces dried rice noodles
2 red chilies, seeded and chopped finely
2 shallots, chopped finely
2 tbsp sugar
2 tbsp tamarind water
1 tbsp lime juice
2 tbsp light soy sauce
1 tbsp sunflower oil
1 tsp sesame oil
6 ounces smoked bean curd, diced pepper
2 tbsp chopped roasted peanuts, to garnish

1 Cook the rice noodles as directed on the packet, or soak them in a large bowl of boiling water for 5 minutes.

2 Grind together the chilies, shallots, sugar, tamarind water, lime juice, light soy sauce, and pepper to taste.

3 Heat both of the oils together in a wok or large, heavy skillet over a high heat. Add the bean curd and stir for 1 minute.

4 Add the chili mixture, bring to a boil, and stir for about 2 minutes until thickened.

5 Drain the rice noodles and add them to the chili mixture. Use 2 spoons to lift and toss them until they are no longer steaming. Serve immediately, garnished with the chopped roasted peanuts.

Grains & Legumes

Grains are the seeds of cultivated grasses, while legumes are the dried seeds of pod-bearing plants of the Leguminosae family. Together they are the most universally important staple foods. Grains include wheat, corn, barley, rye, oats, buckwheat, and many varieties of rice, as well as associated flours. Legumes include garbanzo beans, yellow and green split peas, a fascinating variety of beans, together with many types of lentil.

Grains and legumes form a substantial base to which other ingredients can be added. Each has its own distinctive flavor and texture, so it's worth experimenting with less well-known varieties. An excellent source of protein, iron, calcium, and B vitamins, these valuable foods are cheap, highly nutritious, versatile, and filling, and are virtually fat-free. With the current emphasis on healthier eating, they are a must for the vegetarian diet.

Vegetable Jambalaya

This dish traditionally contains spicy sausage but it is equally delicious
filled with vegetables in this spicy vegetarian version.

Serves 4
1/2 cup brown rice
2 tbsp olive oil
2 garlic cloves, crushed
1 red onion, cut into eight
1 eggplant, diced
1 green bell pepper, diced
1³/4 ounces baby corn cobs, halved lengthwise
1/2 cup frozen peas
3¹/2 ounces small broccoli florets
²/3 cup vegetable stock
8 fl ounce can chopped tomatoes
1 tbsp tomato paste
1 tsp creole seasoning
1/2 tsp chili flakes
salt and pepper

1 Cook the rice in a saucepan of boiling water for 20 minutes or until cooked through. Drain thoroughly and set aside until required.

2 Heat the oil in a heavy-based skillet and cook the garlic and onion for 2–3 minutes, stirring.

3 Add the eggplant, bell pepper, corn, peas, and broccoli to the pan and cook, stirring occasionally, for 2–3 minutes.

4 Stir in the stock and canned tomatoes, tomato paste, creole seasoning, and chili flakes. Season with salt and pepper to taste and cook over a low heat for 15–20 minutes or until the vegetables are tender.

5 Stir the brown rice into the vegetable mixture and cook, mixing well, for 3–4 minutes or until hot.

6 Transfer the vegetable jambalaya to warm serving dishes and serve immediately.

COOK'S TIP

Use a mixture of rice, such as wild or red rice, for color and texture. Cook the rice in advance for a speedier recipe.

Mushroom & Parmesan Risotto

Make this creamy risotto with Italian arborio rice
and freshly grated Parmesan for the best results.

Serves 4
2 tbsp olive or vegetable oil
generous 1 cup arborio rice
2 garlic cloves, crushed
1 onion, chopped
2 celery stalks, chopped
1 red or green bell pepper, deseeded and chopped
9 ounces mushrooms, sliced
1 tbsp chopped fresh oregano or 1 tsp dried oregano
4 cups Fresh Vegetable Stock (see page 14)
2 ounces sun-dried tomatoes in olive oil, drained and chopped (optional)
1/2 cup freshly grated Parmesan
salt and pepper
TO GARNISH
fresh flat-leaf parsley sprigs
fresh bay leaves

1 Heat the oil in a wok or large skillet. Add the rice and cook, stirring, for 5 minutes.

2 Add the garlic, onion, celery, and bell pepper and cook, stirring, for 5 minutes. Add the mushrooms and cook for a further 3–4 minutes.

3 Stir in the oregano and stock. Heat until just boiling, then reduce the heat, cover, and simmer gently for about 20 minutes until the rice is tender and creamy.

4 Add the sun-dried tomatoes, if using, and season with salt and pepper to taste. Stir in half the Parmesan. Top with the remaining cheese, and garnish with flat-leaf parsley and bay leaves. Serve.

COOK'S TIP

Add the stock a little at a time, only adding more when the last addition is fully absorbed.

Lentil Croquettes

These croquettes are ideal served with a crisp salad and a
sesame seed paste dip.

Serves 4
1¹/₄ cups split red lentils
1 green bell pepper, finely chopped
1 red onion, finely chopped
2 garlic cloves, crushed
1 tsp garam masala
¹/₂ tsp chili powder
1 tsp ground cumin
2 tsp lemon juice
2 tbsp chopped unsalted peanuts
2¹/₂ cups water
1 egg, beaten
3 tbsp all-purpose flour
1 tsp turmeric
1 tsp chili powder
4 tbsp vegetable oil
salt and pepper
salad leaves and fresh herbs, to serve

1 Put the lentils in a large saucepan with the bell pepper, onion, garlic, garam masala, chili powder, ground cumin, lemon juice, and peanuts.

2 Add the water and bring to a boil. Reduce the heat and simmer for 30 minutes or until the liquid has been absorbed, stirring occasionally.

3 Remove the mixture from the heat and leave to cool slightly. Beat in the egg and season with salt and pepper to taste. Leave to cool completely.

4 With floured hands, form the mixture into eight oblong shapes.

5 Mix the flour, turmeric, and chili powder together on a small plate. Roll the croquettes in the spiced flour mixture to coat.

6 Heat the oil in a large skillet and cook the croquettes, in batches, for 10 minutes, turning once, until crisp on both sides. Serve.

COOK'S TIP

Other lentils could be used, but they will require soaking and precooking before use. Red lentils are used for speed and convenience.

Oriental-style Millet Pilau

Millet makes an interesting alternative to rice, which is the more traditional ingredient for a pilau. Serve with a crisp salad of oriental vegetables.

Serves 4
1¹/₂ cups millet grains
1 tbsp vegetable oil
1 bunch scallions, white and green parts, chopped
1 garlic clove, crushed
1 tsp grated ginger root
1 orange bell pepper, seeded and diced
2¹/₂ cups water
1 orange
²/₃ cup chopped pitted dates
2 tsp sesame oil
1 cup roasted cashew nuts
2 tbsp pumpkin seeds
salt and pepper
oriental salad vegetables, to serve

1 Place the millet in a large saucepan and cook over a medium heat for 4–5 minutes to toast, shaking the pan occasionally, until the grains begin to crack and pop.

2 Heat the oil in a separate saucepan and gently fry the scallions, garlic, ginger, and bell pepper for 2–3 minutes until just softened but not browned. Add the millet and pour in the water.

3 Using a vegetable peeler, pare the rind from the orange and add the rind to the pan. Squeeze the juice from the orange into the pan. Season well.

4 Bring the mixture to a boil, reduce the heat, cover, and cook gently for

20 minutes or until all of the liquid has been absorbed. Remove the pan from the heat, stir in the dates and sesame oil, and leave to stand for 10 minutes.

5 Discard the orange rind and stir in the cashew nuts. Transfer to a serving dish, sprinkle with pumpkin seeds, and serve with oriental salad vegetables.

Brown Rice, Vegetable, & Herb Gratin

This is a really filling dish and therefore does not require an accompaniment.
It is very versatile, and could be made with a wide selection of vegetables.

Serves 4
$\frac{1}{3}$ cup brown rice
2 tbsp butter or vegetarian margarine
1 red onion, chopped
2 garlic cloves, crushed
1 carrot, cut into matchsticks
1 zucchini, sliced
$2\frac{3}{4}$ ounces baby corn cobs, halved lengthwise
2 tbsp sunflower seeds
3 tbsp chopped mixed herbs
1 cup grated Mozzarella cheese
2 tbsp whole wheat bread crumbs
salt and pepper

1 Cook the rice in a saucepan of boiling, salted water for 20 minutes or until cooked. Drain well.

2 Lightly grease a 1½ pint ovenproof dish.

3 Heat the butter in a skillet. Add the onion and cook, stirring, for 2 minutes or until softened.

4 Add the garlic, carrot, zucchini, and corn cobs and cook for a further 5 minutes, stirring.

5 Mix the rice with the sunflower seeds and mixed herbs and stir into the pan.

6 Stir in half of the Mozzarella cheese and season with salt and pepper to taste.

7 Spoon the mixture into the greased dish and top with the bread crumbs and remaining cheese. Cook in a preheated oven at 350°F for 25–30 minutes or until the cheese begins to turn golden. Serve.

COOK'S VARIATION

Use an alternative rice, such as basmati, and flavor the dish with curry spices, if you prefer.

Chatuchak Fried Rice

An excellent way to use up leftover rice. Pop it into the freezer
as soon as it is cool, and it will be ready to reheat at any time.

Serves 4
1 tbsp sunflower oil
2 garlic cloves, crushed
1 inch piece ginger root, shredded finely
3 shallots, chopped finely
1 red chili, seeded and chopped finely
1/2 green bell pepper, seeded and sliced finely
2–3 baby eggplants, quartered
3 ounces sugar snap peas or snow peas, trimmed and blanched
6 baby corn cobs, halved lengthwise and blanched
1 tomato, cut into 8 pieces
3 ounces bean sprouts
3 cups cooked Thai jasmine rice
2 tbsp ketchup
2 tbsp light soy sauce
TO GARNISH
fresh cilantro leaves
lime wedges

1 Heat the sunflower oil in a wok
or large, heavy skillet over a high
heat. Add the garlic and ginger,
stirring well.

2 Add the shallots, chili, green
bell pepper, and baby eggplants and
cook, stirring, until the shallots have
softened. Add the sugar snap peas or
snow peas, corn cobs, tomato, and
bean sprouts and cook, stirring, for
3 minutes.

3 Add the rice, and lift and mix with
two spoons for 4–5 minutes, until no
more steam is released. Stir in the
ketchup and soy sauce.

4 Transfer to serving dishes and serve
immediately, garnished with cilantro
leaves and lime wedges to squeeze
over the rice.

Moroccan Vegetable Couscous

Couscous is a semolina grain which is very quick to cook,
and it makes a pleasant change from rice or pasta.

Serves 4
2 tbsp vegetable oil
1 large onion, chopped coarsely
1 carrot, chopped
1 turnip, chopped
2¹/₂ cups Fresh Vegetable Stock (see page 14)
1 cup couscous
2 tomatoes, peeled and quartered
2 zucchini, chopped
1 red bell pepper, seeded and chopped
4¹/₂ ounces green beans, chopped
grated rind of 1 lemon
pinch of ground turmeric (optional)
1 tbsp finely chopped fresh cilantro or parsley
fresh flat-leaf parsley sprigs, to garnish

1 Heat the oil in a large saucepan and fry the onion, carrot, and turnip for 3–4 minutes. Add the vegetable stock and bring to a boil. Cover and simmer gently for about 20 minutes.

2 Meanwhile, put the couscous in a bowl and moisten with a little boiling water, stirring, until the grains have swollen and separated.

3 Add the tomatoes, zucchini, bell pepper, and green beans to the saucepan, mixing well.

4 Stir the lemon rind and turmeric, if using, into the couscous and mix well. Put the couscous in a steamer and position over the vegetables.

Simmer the vegetables so that the couscous steams for 8–10 minutes.

5 Using a fork, fluff up the couscous and transfer to warmed serving plates.

Ladle the vegetables and some of the liquid over the top of the couscous. Scatter with the cilantro or parsley and serve at once, garnished with parsley sprigs.

Green Lentil & Mixed Vegetable Pan-fry

The green lentils used in this recipe require soaking but are worth it for the flavor.
If time is short, use red split peas which do not require soaking.

Serves 4
3³/₄ cups green lentils
4 tbsp butter or vegetarian margarine
2 garlic cloves, crushed
2 tbsp olive oil
1 tbsp cider vinegar
1 red onion, cut into eight
1³/₄ ounces baby corn cobs, halved lengthwise
1 yellow bell pepper, cut into strips
1 red bell pepper, cut into strips
1³/₄ ounces green beans, halved
6 tbsp vegetable stock
2 tbsp clear honey
salt and pepper

1 Soak the lentils in a large saucepan of cold water for 25 minutes. Bring to a boil, reduce the heat, and simmer for 20 minutes. Drain thoroughly.

2 Add 1 tablespoon of the butter or margarine, 1 garlic clove, 1 tablespoon of oil, and the vinegar to the lentils and mix well.

3 Melt the remaining butter, garlic, and oil in a skillet and stir fry the onion, corn cobs, bell peppers, and beans for 3–4 minutes.

4 Add the stock and bring to a boil for about 10 minutes or until the liquid has evaporated.

5 Add the honey and season with salt and pepper to taste. Stir in the lentil mixture and cook for 1 minute to heat through. Spoon onto warmed serving plates and serve with crusty bread.

Garbanzo Bean & Peanut Balls

These tasty, nutty morsels are delicious served with a fiery, tangy sauce that counteracts the richness of the peanuts.

Serves 4

3 tbsp groundnut oil
1 onion, chopped finely
1 celery stalk, chopped
1 tsp dried mixed herbs
2 cups roasted unsalted peanuts, ground
1 cup canned garbanzo beans, drained and mashed
1 tsp yeast extract
1 cup fresh whole wheat bread crumbs
1 egg yolk
1/4 cup all-purpose flour
strips of fresh red chili, to garnish
boiled rice and green salad leaves, to serve

HOT CHILI SAUCE

2 tsp groundnut oil
1 large red chili, seeded and chopped finely
2 scallions, chopped finely
2 tbsp red wine vinegar
7 ounce can chopped tomatoes
2 tbsp tomato paste
2 tsp superfine sugar
salt and pepper

1 Heat 1 tablespoon of the oil in a skillet and gently fry the onion and celery for 3–4 minutes until softened but not browned.

2 Place all the other ingredients, except for the remaining oil and the flour, in a mixing bowl and add the onion and celery. Mix well.

3 Divide the mixture into 12 portions and roll into balls. Coat with the flour.

4 Heat the remaining oil in a skillet. Add the garbanzo bean balls and cook over a medium heat for 15 minutes, turning frequently, until cooked through and golden. Drain on paper towels.

5 Meanwhile, make the hot chili sauce. Heat the oil in a small skillet and gently fry the chili and scallions for 2–3 minutes. Stir in the remaining ingredients and season with salt and pepper to taste. Bring to a boil and simmer for 5 minutes.

6 Serve the garbanzo bean and peanut balls with the hot chili sauce, rice, and a green salad.

Cashew Nut Paella

Paella traditionally contains chicken and fish, but this recipe is packed with vegetables and nuts for a truly delicious and simple vegetarian dish.

Serves 4
2 tbsp olive oil
1 tbsp butter
1 red onion, chopped
1 cup arborio rice
1 tsp ground turmeric
1 tsp ground cumin
1/2 tsp chili powder
3 garlic cloves, crushed
1 green chili, sliced
1 green bell pepper, diced
1 red bell pepper, diced
2³/4 ounces baby corn cobs, halved lengthwise
2 tbsp pitted black olives
1 large tomato, seeded and diced
2 cups vegetable stock
3/4 cup unsalted cashew nuts
1/4 cup frozen peas
2 tbsp chopped parsley
pinch of cayenne pepper
salt and pepper
fresh herbs, to garnish

1 Heat the oil and butter in a large skillet or paella pan until the butter has melted.

2 Add the onion to the pan and sauté for 2–3 minutes, stirring.

3 Stir in the rice, turmeric, cumin, chili powder, garlic, chili, bell peppers, corn cobs, olives, and tomato and cook over a medium heat for 1–2 minutes, stirring.

4 Pour in the stock and bring the mixture to a boil. Reduce the heat and cook for 20 minutes, stirring.

5 Add the cashew nuts and peas to the mixture in the pan and cook for a further 5 minutes, stirring occasionally. Season with salt and pepper to taste and sprinkle with parsley and cayenne pepper. Transfer to warm serving plates, garnish, and serve immediately.

COOK'S TIP

For authenticity and flavor, use a few saffron strands soaked in a little boiling water instead of the turmeric. Saffron has a lovely, nutty flavor.

Cheesy Semolina Fritters with Apple Relish

Based on a gnocchi recipe, these delicious fritters are accompanied by a fruity homemade relish.

Serves 4
2½ cups milk
1 small onion
1 celery stalk
1 bay leaf
2 cloves
⅔ cup semolina
1 cup grated sharp Cheddar
½ tsp dried mustard powder
2 tbsp all-purpose flour
1 egg, beaten
½ cup dried white bread crumbs
6 tbsp vegetable oil
salt and pepper
celery leaves, to garnish
coleslaw, to serve

RELISH
2 celery stalks, chopped
2 small eating apples, cored and diced finely
½ cup golden raisins
½ cup no-soak dried apricots, chopped
6 tbsp cider vinegar
pinch of ground cloves
½ tsp ground cinnamon

1 Pour the milk into a pan and add the onion, celery, bay leaf, and cloves. Bring to a boil, remove from the heat, and let stand for 15 minutes.

2 Strain the mixture into another pan, bring to a boil, and sprinkle in the semolina, stirring constantly. Reduce the heat and simmer for 5 minutes until very thick, stirring occasionally to prevent it sticking.

3 Remove from the heat and beat in the cheese, mustard, and seasoning. Place in a greased bowl and let cool.

4 To make the relish, put all of the ingredients in a pan, bring to a boil, cover, and simmer for 20 minutes, until tender. Let cool.

5 Put the flour, egg, and bread crumbs onto separate plates. Divide the cooled semolina mixture into eight and press into 2½ inch rounds. Coat the rounds lightly in the flour, then in the egg and bread crumbs. Heat the oil in a large skillet and fry the fritters for 3–4 minutes on each side until golden. Drain on paper towels. Garnish and serve with the relish and coleslaw.

Pesto Rice with Garlic Bread

Try this combination of two types of rice with the richness
of pine nuts, basil, and freshly grated Parmesan.

Serves 4

1½ cups mixed long-grain
and wild rice

fresh basil sprigs, to garnish

tomato and orange salad,
to serve

PESTO DRESSING

½ ounce fresh basil leaves

1 cup pine nuts

2 garlic cloves, crushed

6 tbsp olive oil

½ cup freshly grated Parmesan

salt and pepper

GARLIC BREAD

2 small granary or whole wheat
French bread sticks

½ cup butter or
vegetarian margarine, softened

2 garlic cloves, crushed

1 tsp dried mixed herbs

1 Place the rice in a saucepan and
cover with water. Bring to a boil
and cook according to the packet
instructions. Drain thoroughly, set
aside, and keep warm.

2 Meanwhile, make the pesto
dressing. Remove the basil leaves
from the stalks and finely chop the
leaves. Reserve ¼ cup of the pine
nuts and finely chop the remainder.
Mix with the chopped basil and the
rest of the dressing ingredients.
Alternatively, put all of the
ingredients in a food processor or
blender and blend for a few seconds
until smooth. Set aside.

3 To make the garlic bread, slice the
bread at 1 inch intervals, taking care
not to slice all the way through. Mix
the butter or margarine with the
garlic, herbs, and seasoning. Spread
thickly between each slice.

4 Wrap the bread in foil and bake
in a preheated oven at 400°F for
10–15 minutes.

5 To serve, toast the reserved pine
nuts under a preheated medium
broiler for 2–3 minutes until golden,
Be careful not to burn them. Toss the
pesto dressing into the hot rice and
transfer to a warm serving dish.
Sprinkle with toasted pine nuts and
garnish with basil sprigs. Serve with
the garlic bread and a tomato and
orange salad.

Lentil & Rice Casserole

This is a really hearty dish, perfect for cold days
when a filling hot dish is just what you need.

Serves 4

1$^1/_4$ cups red split lentils
$^1/_3$ cup long-grain white rice
5 cups vegetable stock
$^2/_3$ cup dry white wine
1 leek, cut into chunks
3 garlic cloves, crushed
14 ounce can chopped tomatoes
1 tsp ground cumin
1 tsp chili powder
1 tsp garam masala
1 red bell pepper, sliced
3$^1/_2$ ounces small broccoli florets
8 baby corn cobs, halved lengthwise
1$^3/_4$ ounces green beans, halved
1 tbsp fresh basil, shredded
salt and pepper
fresh basil sprigs, to garnish

1 Place the lentils, rice, stock, and wine in a flameproof casserole dish and cook over a gentle heat for 20 minutes, stirring occasionally.

2 Add the leek, garlic, tomatoes, spices, bell pepper, broccoli, corn cobs, and beans. Bring the mixture to a boil, reduce the heat, cover, and simmer for a further 10–15 minutes or until the vegetables are tender. Add the shredded basil and season to taste. Garnish with fresh basil sprigs and serve immediately.

COOK'S VARIATION

You can vary the rice in this recipe—use brown or wild rice, if you prefer.

Couscous Royale

Serve this stunning dish as a centerpiece for a Moroccan-style feast;
a truly memorable meal.

Serves 4
3 carrots
3 zucchini
12 ounces pumpkin or squash
5 cups Fresh Vegetable Stock (see page 14)
2 cinnamon sticks, broken in half
2 tsp ground cumin
1 tsp ground coriander
pinch of saffron strands
2 tbsp olive oil
pared rind and juice of 1 lemon
2 tbsp clear honey
$2^2/_3$ cups pre-cooked couscous
$^1/_4$ cup butter or vegetarian margarine, softened
1 cup large seedless raisins
salt and pepper
fresh cilantro, to garnish

1 Cut the carrots and zucchini into 3 inch pieces and cut in half lengthwise.

2 Trim the pumpkin or squash and discard the seeds. Peel and cut into 3 inch pieces.

3 Put the stock, spices, saffron, and carrots in a large pan. Bring to a boil, skim off any film, and add the oil. Simmer for 15 minutes. Add the lemon rind and juice to the pan with the honey, zucchini, and pumpkin or squash. Season. Bring back to a boil and simmer for 10 minutes.

4 Soak the couscous according to the packet instructions. Transfer to a steamer or large strainer lined with cheesecloth and place over the vegetable pan. Cover and steam as directed. Stir in the butter.

5 Transfer the couscous to a serving plate. Drain the vegetables, reserving the stock, lemon rind, and cinnamon. Arrange the vegetables on top of the couscous. Sprinkle the raisins on top and spoon over 6 tablespoons of the reserved stock. Keep warm. Return the remaining stock to the heat and boil for 5 minutes to reduce slightly. Discard the lemon rind and cinnamon. Garnish and serve with the sauce.

Vegetable Biryani

The Biryani originated in the North of India and was a dish reserved for festivals. The main ingredient, the vegetables, are marinated in a yogurt-based marinade and cooked in a casserole dish with the rice and onions.

Serves 4
1 large potato, cubed
3½ ounces baby carrots
1¾ ounces okra, thickly sliced
2 celery sticks, sliced
2¾ ounces baby button mushrooms, halved
1 eggplant, halved and sliced
1¼ cups natural yogurt
1 tbsp grated root ginger
2 large onions, grated
4 garlic cloves, crushed
1 tsp turmeric
1 tbsp curry powder
2 tbsp butter
2 onions, sliced
1¼ cups basmati rice
chopped cilantro, to garnish

1 Cook the potato cubes, carrots, and okra in a pan of boiling salted water for 7–8 minutes. Drain well and place in a large bowl. Mix with the celery, mushrooms, and eggplant.

2 Mix the yogurt, ginger, grated onions, garlic, turmeric, and curry powder and pour over the vegetables. Leave to marinate for at least 2 hours.

3 Heat the butter in a skillet and cook the sliced onions for 5–6 minutes until golden brown. Remove a few onions from the pan and reserve for garnishing.

4 Cook the rice in a pan of boiling water for 7 minutes. Drain well.

5 Add the marinated vegetables to the onions and cook for 10 minutes.

6 Put half of the rice in a 3½ pint casserole dish. Spoon the vegetables on top and cover with the remaining rice. Cover and cook in a preheated oven at 375°F for 20–25 minutes or until the rice is tender.

7 Spoon the biryani onto a serving plate, garnish with the reserved onions and chopped cilantro, and serve immediately.

COOK'S VARIATION

Long-grain white rice or brown rice may be used instead of the basmati rice, if you prefer.

Kofta Kabobs with Tabbouleh

Traditionally, koftas are made from a spicy meat mixture, but this bean and wheat version makes a tasty vegetarian alternative.

Serves 4
1 cup aduki beans
1 cup bulgar wheat
scant 2 cups Fresh Vegetable Stock (see page 14)
3 tbsp olive oil
1 onion, chopped finely
2 garlic cloves, crushed
1 tsp ground coriander
1 tsp ground cumin
2 tbsp chopped fresh cilantro
3 eggs, beaten
1 cup dried bread crumbs
salt and pepper

TABBOULEH
1 cup bulgar wheat
2 tbsp lemon juice
1 tbsp olive oil
6 tbsp chopped fresh parsley
4 scallions, chopped finely
2 ounces cucumber, chopped finely
3 tbsp chopped fresh mint
1 extra-large tomato, chopped finely

TO SERVE
Tahini Cream (see page 14)
black olives
pita bread

1 Cook the aduki beans in a pan of boiling water for 40 minutes or until tender. Drain, rinse, and cool. Cook the bulgar wheat in the stock for 10 minutes or until the stock is absorbed.

2 Heat 1 tbsp of the oil in a skillet and fry the onion, garlic, coriander, and cumin for 4–5 minutes. Transfer to a bowl with the beans, cilantro, seasoning, and eggs and mash with a potato masher or fork. Add the bread crumbs and bulgar wheat and stir well. Cover and chill for 1 hour, or until firm.

3 To make the tabbouleh, soak the bulgar wheat in scant 2 cups of boiling water for 15 minutes. Combine with the remaining ingredients. Cover and chill. With wet hands, mold the kofta mixture into 32 oval shapes. Press 4 koftas onto each skewer, brush with oil, and broil for 5–6 minutes until golden. Turn, brush with oil, and cook for 5–6 minutes. Drain on paper towels. Serve with the tabbouleh.

Garbanzo Bean & Vegetable Casserole

Serve this hearty dish with warm crusty bread to mop up the juices.

Serves 4
1 tbsp olive oil
1 red onion, halved and sliced
3 garlic cloves, crushed
8 ounces spinach
1 fennel bulb, cut into eight
1 red bell pepper, cubed
1 tbsp all-purpose flour
$3^3/4$ cups vegetable stock
6 tbsp dry white wine
14 ounce can garbanzo beans, drained
1 bay leaf
1 tsp ground coriander
$^1/_2$ tsp paprika
salt and pepper
fennel fronds, to garnish

1 Heat the oil in a large flameproof casserole dish and sauté the onion and garlic for 1 minute, stirring. Add the spinach and cook for 4 minutes or until wilted.

2 Add the fennel and bell pepper and cook for 2 minutes, stirring. Stir in the flour and cook for 1 minute.

3 Add the stock, wine, garbanzo beans, bay leaf, coriander, and paprika, cover, and cook for 30 minutes. Season to taste, garnish with fennel fronds, and serve immediately.

COOK'S TIP

Use other canned legumes or mixed beans instead of the garbanzo beans, if you prefer.

Deep South Spiced Rice & Beans

Cajun spices add a flavor of the American Deep South
to this colorful rice and red kidney bean salad.

Serves 4
scant 1 cup long-grain rice
4 tbsp olive oil
1 small green bell pepper, seeded and chopped
1 small red bell pepper, seeded and chopped
1 onion, chopped finely
1 small red or green chili, seeded and chopped finely
2 tomatoes, chopped
½ cup canned red kidney beans, rinsed and drained
1 tbsp chopped fresh basil
2 tsp chopped fresh thyme (or 1 tsp dried)
1 tsp Cajun spice
salt and pepper
fresh basil leaves and thyme sprigs, to garnish

1 Cook the rice in a saucepan of boiling, lightly salted water for 12 minutes, or until tender. Rinse with cold water and drain well. Transfer to a large bowl.

2 Meanwhile, heat the olive oil in a skillet. Add the green and red bell peppers and the onion and cook gently for about 5 minutes, or until softened.

3 Add the chili and tomatoes and cook for a further 2 minutes.

4 Add the vegetable mixture and red kidney beans to the rice. Stir well to combine thoroughly.

5 Stir the chopped herbs and Cajun spice into the rice mixture and season with salt and pepper to taste. Transfer to serving plates, garnish with basil leaves and thyme sprigs, and serve.

COOK'S TIP

The fresh red or green chili can be replaced by 1 tsp chili powder.

Vegetable Curry

Vegetables are cooked in a mildly spiced curry sauce with yogurt
and fresh cilantro stirred in just before serving.

Serves 4
2 tbsp sunflower oil
1 onion, sliced
2 tsp cumin seeds
2 tbsp ground coriander
1 tsp ground turmeric
2 tsp ground ginger
1 tsp chopped fresh red chili
2 garlic cloves, chopped
14 ounce can chopped tomatoes
3 tbsp powdered coconut mixed with
1¼ cups boiling water
1 small cauliflower, broken into florets
2 zucchini, sliced
2 carrots, sliced
1 potato, diced
14 ounce can garbanzo beans, drained and rinsed
¾ cup thick natural yogurt
2 tbsp mango chutney
3 tbsp chopped fresh cilantro
salt and pepper
fresh herbs, to garnish

MINT RAITA

⅔ cup natural yogurt
1 tbsp chopped fresh mint

TO SERVE

onion relish
basmati rice
nan bread

1 Heat the oil in a pan and fry the onion until softened. Add the cumin, ground coriander, turmeric, ginger, chili, and garlic and fry for 1 minute.

2 Add the tomatoes and coconut mixture and mix well.

3 Add the cauliflower, zucchini, carrots, potato, garbanzo beans, and seasoning. Cover and simmer for 20 minutes.

4 Stir in the yogurt, mango chutney, and fresh cilantro and heat through gently, but do not boil.

5 To make the mint raita, mix the yogurt and mint. Transfer to a serving dish, then cover, and chill.

6 Transfer the curry to serving plates, garnish with fresh herbs, and serve with mint raita, onion relish, basmati rice, and nan bread.

Egg & Garbanzo Bean Curry

This easy vegetarian curry is always enjoyed. Double the quantities
for a great dish if you're cooking for a crowd.

Serves 4
2 tbsp vegetable oil
2 garlic cloves, crushed
1 large onion, chopped
1 large carrot, sliced
1 apple, cored and chopped
2 tbsp medium-hot curry powder
1 tsp finely grated ginger root
2 tsp paprika
3½ cups Fresh Vegetable Stock (see page 14)
2 tbsp tomato paste
½ small cauliflower, broken into florets
1 pound 1 ounce can garbanzo beans, rinsed and drained
2 tbsp golden raisins or raisins
2 tbsp cornstarch
2 tbsp water
4 hard-boiled eggs, quartered
salt and pepper
paprika, to garnish

CUCUMBER DIP

3 inch piece cucumber, chopped finely
1 tbsp chopped fresh mint
⅔ cup natural yogurt
sprigs of fresh mint, to garnish

1 Heat the oil in a large pan and fry
the garlic, onion, carrot, and apple for
4–5 minutes, until softened. Add the
curry powder, ginger, and paprika and
fry for 1 minute. Stir in the vegetable
stock and tomato paste.

2 Add the cauliflower, garbanzo
beans, and golden raisins or raisins.
Bring to a boil, reduce the heat, and
simmer, covered, for 25–30 minutes
or until tender.

3 Blend the cornstarch with the
water and add to the curry, stirring
until thickened. Cook gently for
2 minutes. Season with salt and
pepper to taste.

4 To make the dip, mix together the
cucumber, mint, and yogurt. Garnish
with fresh mint.

5 Ladle the curry onto 4 serving
plates. Arrange the eggs on top and
sprinkle with a little paprika. Serve
with the cucumber dip.

Risotto Verde

Risotto is an Italian dish which is easy to make and uses arborio rice,
onion, and garlic as a base for a range of savory recipes.

Serves 4
7¹/₂ cups vegetable stock
2 tbsp olive oil
2 garlic cloves, crushed
2 leeks, shredded
1¹/₄ cups arborio rice
1¹/₄ cups dry white wine
4 tbsp mixed chopped herbs
8 ounces baby spinach
3 tbsp natural yogurt
shredded leek, to garnish

1 Pour the stock into a large pan and bring to a boil. Reduce the heat to a simmer. Meanwhile, heat the oil in a separate pan and sauté the garlic and leeks for 2–3 minutes until softened.

2 Stir in the rice and cook for 2 minutes, stirring until well coated.

3 Pour in half of the wine and a little of the hot stock. Cook over a gentle heat until all of the liquid has been absorbed. Add the remaining stock and wine and cook over a low heat for 25 minutes or until the rice is creamy.

4 Stir in the herbs and spinach, season well, and cook for 2 minutes. Stir in the yogurt, garnish, and serve.

COOK'S TIP

Do not hurry the process of cooking the risotto as the rice must absorb the liquid slowly in order for it to reach the correct consistency.

Fried Rice in Pineapple

This has a mild, pleasant flavor and looks very impressive
as part of a party buffet, so everyone can enjoy it.

Serves 4–6
1 large pineapple
1 tbsp sunflower oil
1 garlic clove, crushed
1 small onion, diced
$^1/_2$ celery stalk, sliced
1 tsp coriander seeds, ground
1 tsp cumin seeds, ground
$5^1/_2$ ounces button mushrooms, sliced
$1^1/_3$ cups cooked rice
2 tbsp light soy sauce
$^1/_2$ tsp sugar
$^1/_2$ tsp salt
$^1/_4$ cup cashew nuts

TO GARNISH

1 scallion, sliced finely
fresh cilantro leaves
fresh mint sprig

1 Using a sharp knife, cut the pineapple in half lengthwise and scoop out the flesh to make 2 boat-shaped shells. Cut the flesh into even-size cubes and reserve $4^1/_2$ ounces to use in this recipe. (Any remaining pineapple cubes can be served separately).

2 Heat the oil in a wok or large, heavy skillet.

3 Add the garlic, onion, and celery and cook over a high heat, stirring constantly, for 2 minutes, until softened.

4 Stir in the coriander and cumin seeds, and the mushrooms.

5 Add the pineapple cubes and cooked rice to the pan and stir well. Stir in the soy sauce, sugar, salt, and cashew nuts.

6 Using two spoons, lift and stir the rice for about 4 minutes until it is thoroughly heated through.

7 Spoon the rice mixture into the pineapple boats. Garnish and serve immediately.

Indonesian Hot Rice Salad

Nutty brown rice combines well with peanuts and a sweet and sour mixture
of fruit and vegetables in this tangy combination.

Serves 4
1¹/₂ cups brown rice
14 ounce can pineapple pieces in natural juice, drained
1 bunch scallions, chopped
1 red bell pepper, deseeded and chopped
4¹/₂ ounces bean sprouts
³/₄ cup dry-roasted peanuts
4¹/₂ ounces radishes, sliced thinly

DRESSING

2 tbsp crunchy peanut butter
1 tbsp groundnut oil
2 tbsp light soy sauce
2 tbsp white wine vinegar
2 tsp clear honey
1 tsp chili powder
¹/₂ tsp garlic salt
pepper

1 Put the rice in a saucepan and cover with water. Bring to a boil, then cover, and simmer for 30 minutes until the rice is tender.

2 Meanwhile, make the dressing. Place all of the ingredients in a small bowl and whisk for a few seconds until well combined.

3 Drain the rice and place in a heatproof bowl. Heat the dressing in a small saucepan for 1 minute and then toss into the rice and mix well.

4 Working quickly, stir in the pineapple, scallions, bell pepper, bean sprouts, and peanuts, mixing well to combine.

5 Transfer the rice salad to a warmed serving dish. Arrange the radish slices around the outside and serve immediately.

COOK'S TIP

Peanut butter is nutritious and can be used to flavor and thicken a wide range of sauces and dressings.

Red Bell Peppers Stuffed with Rice

Stuffed bell peppers are a well-known dish, but this
is a new version adapted for the barbecue.

Serves 4
2 red bell peppers, halved lengthwise and seeded
2 tomatoes, halved
2 zucchini, sliced thinly lengthwise
1 red onion, cut into 8 sections, each section held together by the root
4 tbsp olive oil
2 tbsp fresh thyme leaves
$1/3$ cup mixed basmati and wild rice, cooked
salt and pepper

1 Put the bell peppers, tomatoes, zucchini, and onion sections onto a cookie sheet. Brush the vegetables with olive oil and sprinkle over the fresh thyme leaves.

2 Cook the bell pepper, onion, and zucchini over a medium hot barbecue for about 6 minutes, turning once. Cook the tomato halves for 2–3 minutes only; remove the tomatoes from the barbecue, set aside, and keep warm.

3 When the bell peppers are cooked, put a spoonful of the cooked rice into each one. Season with plenty of salt and pepper and serve with the tomatoes, zucchini, and onions.

Stir-fries & Sautés

Whether you're cooking a Chinese-style meal or any other kind of dish, stir-frying is one of the most convenient and nutritious ways of cooking vegetarian food. The food is cooked quickly over a very high heat in very little oil. The high heat seals in the natural juices and helps preserve nutrients. The short cooking time makes the vegetables more succulent and preserves texture as well as the natural flavor and color.

A round-bottomed wok is ideal for stir-frying as it conducts and retains heat evenly. The conical shape requires far less oil and the food always returns to the center where the heat is most intense, however vigorously you stir.

Sautéing requires a flat-bottomed pan so that the food can be tossed and stirred without being too crowded. A brisk heat is essential so that the food turns golden and crisp. If you use a non-stick pan you can cut down on the amount of oil required.

Cabbage & Walnut Stir-Fry

This is a really quick, one-pan dish using white
and red cabbage for color and flavor.

Serves 4
12 ounces white cabbage
12 ounces red cabbage
4 tbsp peanut oil
1 tbsp walnut oil
2 garlic cloves, crushed
8 scallions, trimmed
8 ounces firm bean curd, cubed
2 tbsp lemon juice
3$^{1}/_{2}$ ounces walnut halves
2 tsp Dijon mustard
2 tsp poppy seeds
salt and pepper

1 Using a sharp knife, shred the
white and red cabbages thinly and set
aside until required.

2 Heat the peanut and walnut oils
in a preheated wok. Add the garlic,
cabbage, scallions, and bean curd and
cook for 5 minutes, stirring.

3 Add the lemon juice, walnuts, and
mustard, season with salt and pepper,
and cook for a further 5 minutes or
until the cabbage is tender.

4 Transfer the stir-fry to a warm
serving bowl, sprinkle with poppy
seeds, and serve.

COOK'S VARIATION

Sesame seeds could be used instead
of the poppy seeds and drizzle
1 teaspoon of sesame oil over the
dish just before serving, if you wish.

Bean Curd & Vegetable Stir-Fry

This is a quick dish to prepare, making it ideal as a mid-week supper dish, after a busy day at work!

Serves 4
6 ounces potatoes, cubed
1 tbsp olive oil
1 red onion, sliced
8 ounces firm bean curd, diced
2 zucchini, diced
8 canned artichoke hearts, halved
$^2/_3$ cup sieved tomatoes
1 tsp superfine sugar
2 tbsp chopped basil
salt and pepper

1 Cook the potatoes in a saucepan of boiling water for 10 minutes. Drain thoroughly.

2 Heat the oil in a large skillet and sauté the red onion for 2 minutes, stirring.

3 Stir in the bean curd and zucchini and cook for 3–4 minutes until they begin to brown slightly. Add the potatoes, stirring to mix.

4 Stir in the artichoke hearts, sieved tomatoes, sugar, and basil, season with salt and pepper and cook for a further 5 minutes, stirring well. Transfer to serving dishes and serve immediately.

COOK'S VARIATION

Eggplants could be used instead of the zucchini, if preferred.

Red Curry with Cashew Nuts

This is a wonderfully quick dish to prepare. If you don't have time to prepare the curry paste, it can be bought ready-made (use 3 tablespoons for this recipe).

Serves 4
1 cup coconut milk
1 kaffir lime leaf, mid-rib removed
$^1/_4$ tsp light soy sauce
4 baby corn cobs, halved lengthwise
$4^1/_2$ ounces broccoli florets
$4^1/_2$ ounces green beans, cut into 2 inch pieces
$^1/_4$ cup cashew nuts
15 fresh basil leaves
1 tbsp chopped fresh cilantro
1 tbsp chopped roasted peanuts, to garnish
cooked rice, to serve

RED CURRY PASTE

7 fresh red chilies, halved, seeded, and blanched (use dried if fresh are not available)
2 tsp cumin seeds
2 tsp coriander seeds
1 inch piece galangal, peeled and chopped
$^1/_2$ stalk lemon grass, chopped
1 tsp salt
grated rind of 1 lime
4 garlic cloves, chopped
3 shallots, chopped
2 kaffir lime leaves, mid-rib removed, shredded
1 tbsp oil to blend

1 To make the red curry paste, grind the chilies, cumin, coriander, galangal, lemon grass, salt, lime, garlic, shallots, and lime leaves in a pestle and mortar, food processor, or grinder. Blend with the oil. The paste will keep for up to 3 weeks in a sealed jar in the refrigerator.

2 Preheat a wok or large, heavy skillet, add 3 tablespoons of the red curry paste, and cook over a high heat, stirring, until fragrant.

3 Reduce the heat and add the coconut milk, lime leaf, light soy sauce, corn cobs, broccoli, beans, and cashew nuts. Bring to a boil and simmer for about 10 minutes until the vegetables are cooked, but still firm.

4 Remove the lime leaf and stir in the basil leaves and cilantro. Garnish with peanuts and serve with cooked rice.

Three Mushrooms in Coconut Milk

A filling and tasty main course dish served over rice or noodles.

Serves 4

2 lemon grass stalks, sliced thinly
2 green chilies, seeded and chopped finely
1 tbsp light soy sauce
2 garlic cloves, crushed
2 tbsp chopped fresh cilantro
2 tbsp chopped fresh parsley
6 slices galangal, peeled
3 tbsp sunflower oil
1 eggplant, cubed
2 ounces oyster mushrooms
2 ounces chestnut mushrooms
2 ounces field mushrooms, quartered if large
4 1/2 ounces green beans, cut into 2 inch lengths, blanched
1 1/4 cups coconut milk
1 tbsp lemon juice
fresh cilantro sprigs to garnish
cooked rice, to serve

1 Grind the lemon grass, chilies, soy sauce, garlic, cilantro, parsley and galangal in a large pestle and mortar or a food processor. Set aside until required.

2 Heat the sunflower oil in a preheated wok or large, heavy skillet. Add the eggplant and stir over a high heat for 3 minutes. Stir in the mushrooms and beans and cook for 3 minutes, stirring constantly. Add the ground spice paste, stirring to mix.

3 Add the coconut milk and lemon juice to the pan, bring to a boil, and simmer for 2 minutes.

4 Serve immediately with rice, and garnish with fresh cilantro.

COOK'S TIP

Any mixture of tasty mushrooms can be used in this recipe. You can even use dried mushrooms.

Cantonese Garden Vegetable Stir-Fry

This dish tastes as fresh as it looks. Try to get hold of baby vegetables as
they look and taste so much better in this dish.

Serves 4
2 tbsp peanut oil
1 tsp Chinese five-spice powder
$2^3/_4$ ounces baby carrots, halved
2 celery sticks, sliced
2 baby leeks, sliced
$1^3/_4$ ounces snow peas
4 baby zucchini, halved lengthwise
8 baby corn cobs
8 ounces firm marinated bean curd, cubed
4 tbsp fresh orange juice
1 tbsp clear honey
celery leaves and orange zest, to garnish
cooked rice or noodles, to serve

1 Heat the oil in a preheated wok until almost smoking. Add the Chinese five-spice powder, carrots, celery, leeks, snow peas, zucchini, and corn cobs and stir-fry for 3–4 minutes.

2 Add the bean curd and cook for a further 2 minutes, stirring.

3 Stir in the orange juice and honey, reduce the heat, and cook for 1–2 minutes. Garnish with celery leaves and orange zest and serve with rice or noodles.

COOK'S VARIATION

Lemon juice would be just as delicious as the orange juice in this recipe, but use 3 tablespoons instead of 4 tablespoons.

Stir-Fried Greens

This is an easy recipe to make as a quick accompaniment to a main course.
The water chestnuts give a delicious crunch to the greens.

Serves 4
1 tbsp sunflower oil
1 garlic clove, halved
2 scallions, sliced finely
7 ounce can water chestnuts, drained and sliced finely (optional)
1 pound 2 ounces spinach, tough stalks removed
1 tsp sherry vinegar
1 tsp light soy sauce
pepper

1 Heat the oil in a preheated wok or large, heavy skillet over a high heat.

2 Add the garlic and cook, stirring, for 1 minute. Be careful not to let the garlic burn on the bottom of the wok or skillet.

3 Add the scallions and water chestnuts, if using, and stir-fry for 2–3 minutes.

4 Stir in the spinach. Add the sherry vinegar, soy sauce, and a sprinkling of pepper and cook, stirring, until the spinach is tender. Remove the garlic.

5 Transfer the stir-fried greens to a warmed serving dish, using a slotted spoon in order to drain off the excess liquid. Serve immediately.

Sweet & Sour Vegetables & Bean Curd

This dish is ideal served with plain noodles for a filling, Oriental meal.

Serves 4
1 tbsp peanut oil
2 garlic cloves, crushed
1 tsp grated root ginger
1³/₄ ounces baby corn cobs
1³/₄ ounces snow peas
1 carrot, cut into matchsticks
1 green bell pepper, cut into matchsticks
8 scallions, trimmed
1³/₄ ounces canned bamboo shoots
8 ounces marinated firm bean curd, cubed
2 tbsp dry sherry
2 tbsp rice vinegar
2 tbsp clear honey
1 tbsp light soy sauce
²/₃ cup vegetable stock
1 tbsp cornstarch

1 Heat the oil in a preheated wok until almost smoking. Add the garlic and ginger and cook for 30 seconds.

2 Add the corn cobs, snow peas, carrot, and bell pepper and stir-fry for 5 minutes or until the vegetables are tender.

3 Add the scallions, bamboo shoots, and bean curd and cook for a further 2 minutes.

4 Stir in the sherry, rice vinegar, honey, soy sauce, vegetable stock, and cornstarch, and bring to a boil. Reduce the heat and simmer for 2 minutes. Transfer to serving dishes and serve.

Stir-Fried Winter Vegetables with Cilantro

Ordinary winter vegetables are given extraordinary treatment in this lively stir-fry, just the thing for perking up jaded palates.

Serves 4

3 tbsp sesame oil
¼ cup blanched almonds
1 large carrot, cut into thin strips
1 large turnip, cut into thin strips
1 onion, sliced finely
1 garlic clove, crushed
3 celery sticks, sliced finely
4½ ounces Brussels sprouts, trimmed and halved
4½ ounces cauliflower, broken into florets
4½ ounces white cabbage, shredded
2 tsp sesame seeds
1 tsp grated fresh root ginger
½ tsp medium chili powder
1 tbsp chopped fresh cilantro
1 tbsp light soy sauce
salt and pepper
sprigs of fresh cilantro, to garnish

1 Heat the sesame oil in a preheated wok or large skillet. Add the almonds and stir-fry until lightly browned. Remove the almonds with a slotted spoon and drain well on paper towels.

2 Add all the vegetables to the wok or skillet, except for the cabbage. Stir-fry briskly for 3–4 minutes.

3 Add the cabbage, sesame seeds, ginger, and chili powder to the vegetables and cook, stirring, for 2 minutes.

4 Add the chopped cilantro, soy sauce, salt and pepper to taste, and the almonds to the mixture, stirring gently. Garnish the vegetables with a few of sprigs of fresh cilantro and serve immediately.

COOK'S TIP

Pumpkin or poppy seeds can be used instead of the sesame seeds. Pumpkin seeds are a good source of zinc.

Green Curry with Tempeh

Green curry paste will keep for up to 3 weeks in the refrigerator. If you don't have time to make the green curry paste, it can be bought ready-made (use 6 tablespoons for this recipe).

Serves 4
1 tbsp sunflower oil
6 ounces marinated or plain tempeh, cut into diamonds
6 scallions, cut into 1 inch pieces
$^2/_3$ cup coconut milk
grated rind of 1 lime
$^1/_4$ cup fresh basil leaves
$^1/_4$ tsp liquid seasoning, such as Maggi

GREEN CURRY PASTE

2 tsp coriander seeds
1 tsp cumin seeds
1 tsp black peppercorns
4 large green chilies, deseeded and chopped
2 shallots, quartered
2 garlic cloves, peeled
2 tbsp chopped fresh cilantro, including root and stalk
grated rind of 1 lime
1 tbsp roughly chopped galangal
1 tsp ground turmeric
salt
2 tbsp oil

TO GARNISH

fresh cilantro leaves
2 green chilies, sliced thinly

1 To make the curry paste, grind the coriander, cumin seeds, and the peppercorns in a food processor or pestle and mortar. Blend the remaining ingredients together and add to the ground spice mixture.

2 Heat the oil in a wok or skillet. Add the tempeh and stir-fry over a high heat for about 2 minutes or until sealed on all sides. Add the scallions and stir-fry for 1 minute. Remove the tempeh and scallions and reserve.

3 Put half of the coconut milk into the wok or skillet and bring to a boil. Add 6 tbsp of the curry paste and the lime rind, and cook for 1 minute. Add the reserved tempeh and scallions. Add the remaining coconut milk and simmer for 7–8 minutes. Stir in the basil leaves and liquid seasoning and simmer for 1 minute. Garnish with the fresh cilantro leaves and chili slices and serve.

Indonesian Chestnut & Vegetable Stir-Fry with Peanut Sauce

This colorful, spicy stir-fry has an Indonesian influence, with the shallots, chilies, ginger, fresh cilantro, and lime.

Serves 4
PEANUT SAUCE
1 cup unsalted roasted peanuts
2 tsp hot chili sauce
3/4 cup coconut milk
2 tbsp soy sauce
1 tbsp ground coriander
pinch of ground turmeric
1 tbsp dark muscovado sugar
STIR-FRY
3 tbsp sesame oil
3–4 shallots, finely sliced
1 garlic clove, finely sliced
1–2 red chilies, seeded and finely chopped
1 large carrot, cut into fine strips
1 yellow and 1 red bell pepper, sliced
1 zucchini, cut into fine strips
4 1/2 ounces sugar-snap peas, trimmed
3 inch piece of cucumber, cut into strips
9 ounces oyster mushrooms
9 ounces canned chestnuts, drained
2 tsp grated ginger root
finely grated rind and juice of 1 lime
1 tbsp chopped fresh cilantro
salt and pepper

1 To make the sauce, grind the peanuts in a blender, or chop very finely. Put into a small pan with the remaining ingredients. Heat gently and simmer for 3–4 minutes.

2 Heat the oil in a wok or skillet. Add the shallots, garlic, and chilies and stir-fry for 2 minutes.

3 Add the carrot, bell peppers, zucchini, and sugar-snap peas to the wok or skillet and stir-fry for 2 minutes.

4 Add the cucumber, mushrooms, chestnuts, ginger, lime rind and juice, cilantro, and salt and pepper to taste to the wok or skillet and stir-fry briskly for about 5 minutes, or until the vegetables are crisp, yet crunchy.

5 Divide the stir-fry between 4 warmed serving plates and serve with the peanut sauce.

Cauliflower with Oriental Greens

This is a delicious way to cook cauliflower—even without the greens.

Serves 4
6 ounces cauliflower, cut into florets
1 garlic clove
$\frac{1}{2}$ tsp turmeric
1 tbsp cilantro root or stem
1 tbsp sunflower oil
2 scallions, cut into 1 inch pieces
$4\frac{1}{2}$ ounces oriental greens, such as Thai spinach, bok choy, or mustard greens, tough stalks removed
1 tsp yellow mustard seeds

1 Blanch the cauliflower, rinse in cold running water, and drain thoroughly. Set aside until required.

2 Grind the garlic, turmeric, and cilantro root or stem together in a pestle and mortar or spice grinder.

3 Heat the oil in a wok or large, heavy skillet. Add the scallions and stir-fry over a high heat for 2 minutes. Add the greens and stir-fry for 1 minute. Remove and set aside.

4 Return the wok or skillet to the heat. Add the mustard seeds and stir-fry until they start to pop. Add the turmeric mixture and the cauliflower and stir-fry until the cauliflower is coated.

5 Transfer to a warmed serving plate and serve with the greens.

Kidney Bean Kiev

This is a vegetarian version of chicken kiev, the bean patties taking the place of the chicken. Topped with garlic and herb butter and coated in bread crumbs, this version is just as delicious.

Serves 4
GARLIC BUTTER
8 tbsp butter
3 garlic cloves, crushed
1 tbsp chopped parsley
BEAN PATTIES
1 pound 7 ounces canned red kidney beans
1¹/₄ cups fresh white bread crumbs
2 tbsp butter
1 leek, chopped
1 celery stick, chopped
1 tbsp chopped parsley
1 egg, beaten
salt and pepper
vegetable oil, for shallow frying

1 To make the garlic butter, put the butter, garlic, and parsley in a bowl and blend together with a wooden spoon. Place the garlic butter mixture onto a sheet of greaseproof paper, roll into a cigar shape, and wrap in the greaseproof paper. Leave to chill in the refrigerator.

2 Using a potato masher, mash the beans in a mixing bowl and stir in ³/₄ cup of the bread crumbs.

3 Melt the butter in a skillet and sauté the leek and celery for 3–4 minutes, stirring.

4 Add the bean mixture to the pan together with the parsley, season with salt and pepper to taste, and mix well. Remove from the heat and leave to cool slightly.

5 Shape the bean mixture into 4 equal sized ovals.

6 Slice the garlic butter into 4 and place a slice in the center of each bean patty. Mold the bean mixture around the garlic butter to encase it completely.

7 Dip each bean patty into the beaten egg to coat and then roll in the remaining bread crumbs.

8 Heat a little oil in a skillet and fry the patties, turning once, for 7–10 minutes or until golden. Serve immediately.

Vegetable Chop Suey

A classic Chinese dish found on all take-out menus,
this recipe is quick to prepare and makes a tasty meal.

Serves 4
2 tbsp peanut oil
1 onion, chopped
3 garlic cloves, chopped
1 green bell pepper, diced
1 red bell pepper, diced
$2^3/_4$ ounces broccoli florets
1 zucchini, sliced
1 ounce green beans
1 carrot, cut into matchsticks
$3^1/_2$ ounces bean sprouts
2 tsp light brown sugar
2 tbsp light soy sauce
$^1/_2$ cup vegetable stock
salt and pepper

1 Heat the oil in a preheated wok until almost smoking. Add the onion and garlic and stir-fry for 30 seconds.

2 Stir in the bell peppers, broccoli, zucchini, beans, and carrot and stir-fry for a further 2–3 minutes.

3 Add the bean sprouts, sugar, soy sauce, vegetable stock, and salt and pepper to taste and cook for about 2 minutes.

4 Transfer to serving plates and serve immediately with noodles.

COOK'S TIP

Ensure that the vegetable pieces are of the same size in order that they all cook in the stated time.

Vegetable & Feta Cheese Patties

Grated carrots, zucchini, and Feta cheese are combined with
cumin seeds, poppy seeds, curry powder, and chopped fresh parsley.

Serves 4
2 large carrots
1 large zucchini
1 small onion
2 ounces Feta cheese
$^1/_4$ cup all-purpose flour
$^1/_4$ tsp cumin seeds
$^1/_2$ tsp poppy seeds
1 tsp medium curry powder
1 tbsp chopped fresh parsley
1 egg, beaten
2 tbsp butter
2 tbsp vegetable oil
salt and pepper
sprigs of fresh herbs, to garnish

1 Grate the carrots, zucchini, onion, and Feta cheese coarsely in a food processor. Alternatively, use a hand-held grater.

2 Mix together the flour, cumin seeds, poppy seeds, curry powder, and parsley in a large bowl. Season well with salt and pepper.

3 Add the vegetable and Feta cheese mixture to the seasoned flour, tossing well to combine. Stir in the beaten egg and mix well.

4 Heat the butter and oil in a large skillet. Place heaped tablespoonfuls of the vegetable and cheese mixture in the pan, flattening them slightly with the back of the spoon. Fry gently for about 2 minutes on each side, until crisp and golden brown. Drain on paper towels and keep warm.

5 Garnish with sprigs of fresh herbs and serve.

COOK'S VARIATION

Omit the cumin and curry powder; use 1 tbsp oregano for the parsley.

Corn & Potato Fritters

An ideal supper dish for two, or for one if you halve the quantities.
You can use the remaining corn in another recipe.

Serves 2
2 tbsp oil
1 small onion, sliced thinly
1 garlic clove, crushed
12 ounces potatoes
7 ounce can corn, drained
$1/2$ tsp dried oregano
1 egg, beaten
$1/2$ cup Edam or Gouda cheese, grated
2–4 eggs
2–4 tomatoes, sliced
salt and pepper
fresh parsley sprigs, to garnish

1 Heat 1 tablespoon of the oil in a non-stick skillet. Add the onion and garlic and fry very gently, stirring frequently, until soft, but only lightly colored. Remove the pan from the heat.

2 Grate the potatoes coarsely into a bowl and mix in the corn, oregano, beaten egg, and salt and pepper. Add the fried onion and garlic and mix well.

3 Heat the remaining oil in the skillet. Divide the potato mixture in half to make two oval-shaped fritters. Add the fritters to the pan, levelling and shaping the fritters with a spatula. Sauté the fritters gently, turning once (making sure that they do not stick to the bottom of the skillet), for about 10 minutes or until browned underneath and almost cooked through. Remove the fritters from the skillet.

4 Sprinkle each fritter with the cheese and place under a preheated medium hot broiler until golden.

5 Meanwhile, poach either one or two eggs for each person until just cooked.

6 Transfer the corn and potato fritters to warmed plates and top each with the eggs and sliced tomatoes.

7 Garnish with fresh parsley and serve at once.

Golden Cheese, Leek, & Potato Cakes

Make these tasty potato cakes for a quick and simple supper dish.
Serve them with scrambled eggs if you're very hungry.

Serves 4
2 pounds 4 ounces potatoes
4 tbsp milk
¼ cup butter
or vegetarian margarine
2 leeks, chopped finely
1 onion, chopped finely
1½ cups grated sharp Cheddar
1 tbsp chopped fresh parsley
or chives
1 egg, beaten
2 tbsp water
1½ cups fresh white
or brown bread crumbs
vegetable oil, for shallow frying
salt and pepper
fresh flat-leaf parsley sprigs,
to garnish
tomato salad and cucumber and
corn relish, to serve

1 Cook the potatoes in a saucepan
of lightly salted, boiling water until
tender. Drain thoroughly. Mash the
potatoes with the milk and the butter
or margarine.

2 Cook the leeks and onion in a small
amount of salted, boiling water for
about 10 minutes until tender. Drain.

3 In a large mixing bowl, combine the
leeks and onion with the mashed
potato, cheese, and parsley or chives.
Season to taste.

4 Beat the egg and water together in a
bowl. Sprinkle the bread crumbs into
a separate bowl.

5 Shape the potato mixture into 12
cakes. Brush each cake with the egg
mixture, then coat in the bread crumbs.

6 Heat the oil in a large skillet and fry
the potato cakes gently, in batches, for
2–3 minutes on each side or until light
golden brown. Garnish with flat-leaf
parsley and serve with a tomato salad
and relish.

Sauté of Summer Vegetables with Tarragon Dressing

The freshness of lightly cooked summer vegetables is enhanced by the aromatic flavor of a tarragon and white wine dressing.

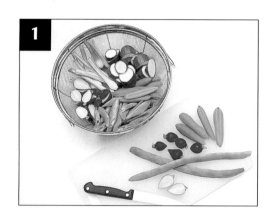

Serves 4
9 ounces baby carrots, scrubbed
4$\frac{1}{2}$ ounces green beans
2 zucchini, trimmed
1 bunch large scallions, trimmed
1 bunch radishes, trimmed
$\frac{1}{2}$ cup butter
2 tbsp light olive oil
2 tbsp white wine vinegar
4 tbsp dry white wine
1 tsp superfine sugar
1 tbsp chopped fresh tarragon
salt and pepper
sprigs of fresh tarragon, to garnish

1 Trim and halve the carrots, slice the beans and zucchini, and halve the scallions and radishes, so that all of the vegetables are cut to even-sized pieces.

2 Melt the butter in a large skillet or wok. Add all of the vegetables and stir-fry over a medium heat, stirring frequently.

3 Heat the olive oil, vinegar, white wine, sugar, and salt and pepper to taste in a small saucepan. Remove from the heat and add the tarragon.

4 When the vegetables are just cooked, but still retain their crunchiness, pour over the "dressing" Stir through, and then transfer to a warmed serving dish. Garnish with sprigs of fresh tarragon and serve at once.

Corn Patties

These are a delicious addition to any party buffet, and are very simple to prepare.
Serve with a sweet chili sauce.

Makes 12
11½ ounce can corn, drained
1 onion, chopped finely
1 tsp curry powder
1 garlic clove, crushed
1 tsp ground coriander
2 scallions, chopped
3 tbsp all-purpose flour
½ tsp baking powder
salt
1 large egg
4 tbsp sunflower oil
scallions, sliced diagonally, to garnish

1 Mash the drained corn lightly in a medium-sized bowl.

2 Add all the remaining ingredients, except for the oil, one at a time, stirring after each addition.

3 Heat the sunflower oil in a skillet. Drop tablespoonfuls of the mixture carefully into the hot oil, far enough apart for them not to run into each other as they cook. Alternatively, cook the patties one at a time. Cook the patties for 4–5 minutes, turning each patty once, until golden brown and firm. Take care not to turn them too soon, or they will break up in the pan.

4 Remove the patties from the pan and drain on paper towels. Serve quickly while still warm.

Bakes & Roasts

Anyone who ever thought that vegetarian meals were dull will be proved very wrong by the rich variety of dishes in this chapter. You'll recognize influences from all over the world, but there are also traditional stews and casseroles as well as hearty bakes and roasts. They all make exciting eating at any time of year, and for virtually any occasion. There are lots of ideas for mid-week meals or for entertaining, some traditional and some more unusual.

Some of the ingredients may be unfamiliar but you should have no difficulty in buying them from health food stores or large supermarkets. Don't be afraid to substitute ingredients where appropriate. There is no reason why you cannot enjoy experimenting and adding your own touch to these imaginative ideas.

Garbanzo Bean Roast with Sherry Sauce

This is a vegetarian version of the classic "Beef Wellington," and just as delicious.
Served with a sherry sauce and roasted vegetables it makes a tasty and impressive main dish.

Serves 4
1 pound can garbanzo beans, drained
1 tsp yeast extract
1¼ cups chopped walnuts
1¼ cups fresh white bread crumbs
1 onion, finely chopped
3½ ounces mushrooms, sliced
1¾ ounces canned corn, drained
2 garlic cloves, crushed
2 tbsp dry sherry
2 tbsp vegetable stock
1 tbsp chopped cilantro
8 ounces prepared puff pastry
1 egg, beaten
2 tbsp milk
salt and pepper
SAUCE
1 tbsp vegetable oil
1 leek, thinly sliced
4 tbsp dry sherry
⅔ cup vegetable stock

1 Put the garbanzo beans, yeast extract, nuts, and bread crumbs in a food processor and blend for 30 seconds. Put the onion and mushrooms in a large skillet and sauté in their own juices for 3–4 minutes.

2 Stir the garbanzo bean mixture into the pan with the corn and garlic. Stir in the sherry, stock, cilantro, and seasoning and bind the mixture together. Remove from the heat and allow to cool.

3 Roll the pastry out onto a lightly floured surface to form a 14 inch × 12 inch rectangle.

4 Shape the garbanzo bean mixture into a loaf shape and wrap the pastry around it, sealing the edges. Place seam-side down on a dampened cookie sheet and score the top in a criss-cross pattern. Mix the egg and milk and brush over the pastry to glaze. Cook in a preheated oven at Gas Mark 6 for 25–30 minutes or until risen and golden. Heat the oil for the sauce in a pan and sauté the leek for 5 minutes, stirring. Add the remaining ingredients and bring to a boil. Simmer for 5 minutes and serve with the roast.

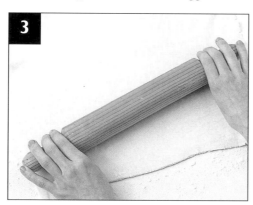

Savory Bread & Butter Pudding

Quick, simple, and nutritious—what more could
you ask for an inexpensive mid-week meal?

Serves 4
¼ cup butter or vegetarian margarine
1 bunch scallions, sliced
6 slices white or brown bread, crusts removed
1½ cups grated sharp Cheddar
2 eggs
scant 2 cups milk
salt and pepper
sprigs of fresh flat-leaf parsley, to garnish

1 Grease a 2¾ pint baking dish with a
little of the butter or margarine. Melt
the remaining butter or margarine in
a small saucepan and fry the scallions
until softened and golden.

2 Cut the bread into triangles and
layer half of them in the baking dish.
Top with the scallions and half of
the cheese.

3 Beat together the eggs and milk and
season with salt and pepper to taste.
Layer the remaining triangles of bread
in the dish and carefully pour over
the milk mixture. Leave to soak for
15–20 minutes.

4 Sprinkle the remaining cheese over
the soaked bread. Bake in a preheated
oven at 375°F for 35–40 minutes or
until puffed up and golden brown.
Garnish with flat-leaf parsley and
serve at once.

Mushroom & Nut Crumble

A filling, tasty dish that is ideal for a warming family supper.
The crunchy topping is flavored with three different types of nuts.

Serves 4
12 ounces open-cap mushrooms, sliced
12 ounces chestnut mushrooms, sliced
1³/₄ cups Fresh Vegetable Stock (see page 14)
¹/₄ cup butter or vegetarian margarine
1 large onion, chopped finely
1 garlic clove, crushed
¹/₂ cup all-purpose flour
4 tbsp heavy cream
2 tbsp chopped fresh parsley
salt and pepper
fresh herbs, to garnish

CRUMBLE TOPPING

³/₄ cup medium oatmeal
³/₄ cup whole wheat flour
¹/₄ cup ground almonds
¹/₄ cup finely chopped walnuts
¹/₂ cup finely chopped unsalted shelled pistachio nuts
1 tsp dried thyme
¹/₃ cup butter or vegetarian margarine, softened
1 tbsp fennel seeds

1 Put the mushrooms and stock in a large saucepan, bring to a boil, cover, and simmer for 15 minutes until tender. Drain the mushrooms, reserving the stock.

2 In another saucepan, melt the butter or margarine and gently fry the onion and garlic for 2–3 minutes until just softened but not browned. Stir in the flour and cook for about 1 minute.

3 Remove the pan from the heat and stir in the reserved stock. Return to the heat and cook, stirring, until thickened. Stir in the mushrooms, seasoning, cream, and parsley and spoon into a shallow ovenproof dish.

4 To make the topping, mix together the oatmeal, flour, nuts, thyme, and plenty of seasoning.

5 Using a fork, mix in the butter or margarine until the topping resembles coarse bread crumbs.

6 Sprinkle the mixture over the mushrooms, sprinkle with fennel seeds, and bake in a preheated oven at 375°F for 25–30 minutes until golden and crisp. Garnish with fresh herbs and serve.

Spicy Potato & Lemon Casserole

This is based on a Moroccan dish in which potatoes are spiced
with cilantro and cumin and cooked in a lemon sauce.

Serves 4
¹/₂ cup olive oil
2 red onions, cut into eight
3 garlic cloves, crushed
2 tsp ground cumin
2 tsp ground coriander
pinch of cayenne pepper
1 carrot, thickly sliced
2 small turnips, quartered
1 zucchini, sliced
1 pound potatoes, thickly sliced
juice and rind of 2 large lemons
1¹/₄ cups vegetable stock
2 tbsp chopped cilantro
salt and pepper

1 Heat the olive oil in a flameproof casserole.

2 Add the red onion and sauté for 3 minutes, stirring.

3 Add the garlic and cook for 30 seconds. Mix in the cumin, ground coriander, and cayenne pepper and cook for 1 minute, stirring.

4 Add the carrot, turnips, zucchini, and potatoes and stir to coat in the oil.

5 Add the lemon juice and rind, stock, and salt and pepper to taste, cover, and cook over a medium heat for 20–30 minutes, stirring occasionally.

6 Remove the lid, sprinkle in the cilantro, and stir well. Serve.

COOK'S TIP

A selection of spices and herbs is important for adding variety to your cooking—add to your range each time you try a new recipe.

COOK'S TIP

Check the vegetables whilst cooking as they may begin to stick to the pan. Add a little more boiling water or stock if necessary.

Lentil Roast

The perfect dish to serve for an alternative Sunday lunch.
Roasted vegetables make a succulent accompaniment.

Serves 6
1 cup red lentils
2 cups Fresh Vegetable Stock (see page 14)
1 bay leaf
1 tbsp butter or vegetarian margarine, softened
2 tbsp dried whole wheat bread crumbs
2 cups grated sharp Cheddar
1 leek, chopped finely
4$^{1}/_{2}$ ounces button mushrooms, chopped finely
1$^{1}/_{2}$ cups fresh whole wheat bread crumbs
2 tbsp chopped fresh parsley
1 tbsp lemon juice
2 eggs, beaten lightly
salt and pepper
sprigs of fresh flat-leaf parsley, to garnish
mixed roasted vegetables, to serve

1 Put the lentils, stock, and bay leaf in a saucepan. Bring to a boil, cover, and simmer gently for 15–20 minutes or until all of the liquid is absorbed and the lentils have softened. Discard the bay leaf.

2 Line the base of a 2 pound 4 ounce loaf pan with baking parchment. Grease the pan with the butter or margarine and sprinkle with the dried bread crumbs.

3 Stir the cheese, leek, mushrooms, fresh bread crumbs, and parsley into the lentils and season with salt and pepper to taste. Bind the mixture together with the lemon juice and eggs.

4 Spoon the mixture into the prepared loaf pan and smooth the top. Bake in a preheated oven at 375°F for 1 hour until golden. Loosen the loaf with a spatula and turn out carefully onto a warmed serving plate. Garnish with parsley and serve sliced with a selection of roasted vegetables.

Vegetable Hot Pot

In this recipe, a variety of vegetables are cooked under a layer of potatoes,
topped with cheese, and cooked until golden brown for a filling and tasty meal.

Serves 4
2 large potatoes, thinly sliced
2 tbsp vegetable oil
1 red onion, halved and sliced
1 leek, sliced
2 garlic cloves, crushed
1 carrot, cut into chunks
3 1/2 ounces broccoli florets
3 1/2 ounces cauliflower florets
2 small turnips, quartered
1 tbsp all-purpose flour
3 1/2 cups vegetable stock
2/3 cup dry cider
1 eating apple, sliced
2 tbsp chopped sage
pinch of cayenne pepper
5 1/2 cups vegetarian Cheddar cheese, grated
salt and pepper

5 Sprinkle the cheese on top of the
potato slices to cover and cook in a
preheated oven at 375°F for 30–35
minutes or until the potato is golden
brown and beginning to crispen
slightly around the edges. Serve
immediately.

COOK'S TIP

If the potato begins to brown too
quickly, cover with foil for the last
10 minutes of cooking time to
prevent the top from burning.

1 Cook the potato slices in a
saucepan of boiling water for 10
minutes. Drain well and reserve.

2 Heat the oil in a flameproof
casserole dish and sauté the onion,
leek, and garlic for 2–3 minutes. Add
the remaining vegetables and cook for
a further 3–4 minutes, stirring.

3 Stir in the flour and cook for
1 minute. Gradually add the stock
and cider and bring the mixture to a
boil. Add the apple, sage, and cayenne
pepper and season well. Remove the
dish from the heat. Transfer the
vegetables to an ovenproof dish.

4 Arrange the potato slices on top
of the vegetable mixture to cover.

Winter Vegetable Cobbler

Seasonal fresh vegetables are casseroled with lentils then topped with
a ring of fresh cheese biscuits to make this tasty cobbler.

Serves 4
1 tbsp olive oil
1 garlic clove, crushed
8 small onions, halved
2 celery stalks, sliced
9 ounces rutabaga, chopped
2 carrots, sliced
½ small cauliflower, broken into florets
9 ounces mushrooms, sliced
14 ounce can chopped tomatoes
¼ cup red lentils
2 tbsp cornstarch
3–4 tbsp water
1¼ cups Fresh Vegetable Stock (see page 14)
2 tsp Tabasco sauce
2 tsp chopped fresh oregano or parsley
sprigs of oregano, to garnish

COBBLER TOPPING
2 cups self-rising flour
¼ cup butter
1 cup grated Cheddar
2 tsp chopped fresh oregano or parsley
1 egg, beaten
⅔ cup skimmed milk
salt

1 Heat the oil in a large pan and fry
the garlic and onions for 5 minutes.
Add the celery, rutabaga, carrots, and
cauliflower and fry for 2–3 minutes.

2 Remove the pan from the heat and
add the mushrooms, tomatoes, and
lentils. Mix the cornstarch with the
water and add to the pan with the
stock, Tabasco sauce, and oregano or
parsley. Bring to a boil, stirring, until

thickened. Transfer to an ovenproof
dish, cover, and bake in a preheated
oven at 350°F for 20 minutes.

3 To make the topping, sift the flour
and a pinch of salt into a bowl. Rub in
the butter, then stir in most of the
cheese and the herbs. Beat the egg and
milk and add enough to the dry

ingredients to make a dough. Knead
and roll out to ½ inch thick. Cut into
2 inch rounds. Remove the dish from
the oven and increase the temperature
to 400°F. Arrange the rounds around the
edge of the dish, brush with the egg and
milk, and sprinkle with the cheese.
Cook for 10–12 minutes. Garnish with
the fresh herbs and serve.

Roast Bell Pepper Tart

This tastes truly delicious, the flavor of roasted vegetables being entirely different from that of boiled or fried.

Serves 8
PASTRY
1¼ cups all-purpose flour
pinch of salt
6 tbsp butter or vegetarian margarine
2 tbsp green pitted olives, finely chopped
3 tbsp cold water
FILLING
1 red bell pepper
1 green bell pepper
1 yellow bell pepper
2 garlic cloves, crushed
2 tbsp olive oil
1 cup Mozzarella cheese, grated
2 eggs
⅔ cup milk
1 tbsp chopped basil
salt and pepper

1 To make the pastry, sieve the flour and a pinch of salt into a mixing bowl. Rub in the butter or margarine until the mixture resembles bread crumbs. Add the olives and cold water, bringing the mixture together to form a dough.

2 Roll the dough out onto a floured surface and use to line an 8 inch loose-bottomed flan pan. Prick the base with a fork and leave to chill.

3 Cut the bell peppers in half lengthwise and lay skin-side uppermost on a cookie sheet. Mix the garlic and oil and brush over the bell peppers. Cook in a preheated oven at 400°F for 20 minutes or until beginning to char slightly. Let cool slightly and thinly slice. Arrange in the base of the pastry case, layering with the Mozzarella cheese. Beat the egg and milk and add the basil. Season and pour over the bell peppers. Put the tart on a cookie sheet and return to the oven for 20–25 minutes or until set. Serve hot or cold.

COOK'S TIP

Make sure that the olives are very finely chopped, otherwise they will make holes in the pastry. They should be almost paste-like in consistency and could be chopped in a food processor for ease and speed.

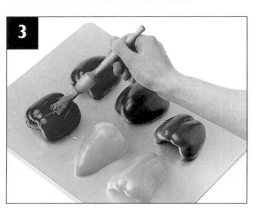

Creamy Baked Fennel

Fennel tastes fabulous in this creamy sauce, flavored with caraway seeds.
A crunchy bread crumb topping gives an interesting change of texture.

Serves 4
2 tbsp lemon juice
2 fennel bulbs, trimmed
$^1/_4$ cup low-fat soft cheese
$^2/_3$ cup light cream
$^2/_3$ cup milk
1 egg, beaten
$^1/_4$ cup butter
2 tsp caraway seeds
1 cup fresh white bread crumbs
salt and pepper
sprigs of flat-leaf parsley, to garnish

1 Bring a large saucepan of water to a boil and add the lemon juice. Slice the bulbs of fennel thinly and add them to the saucepan. Cook for 2–3 minutes to blanch, and then drain.

2 Arrange the slices of fennel in a buttered ovenproof baking dish.

3 Beat the soft cheese in a bowl until smooth. Add the cream, milk, and beaten egg and whisk together until combined. Season with salt and pepper to taste and pour the mixture over the fennel.

4 Melt $^1/_2$ ounce of the butter in a small skillet and fry the caraway seeds gently for 1–2 minutes, to release their flavor and aroma. Sprinkle them over the fennel.

5 Melt the remaining butter in a skillet.

6 Add the bread crumbs to the skillet and fry gently until lightly browned but do not let them burn. Sprinkle the bread crumbs evenly over the surface of the fennel.

7 Cook in a preheated oven at 350°F for 25–30 minutes, or until the fennel is tender. Transfer to serving plates, garnish with sprigs of parsley, and serve.

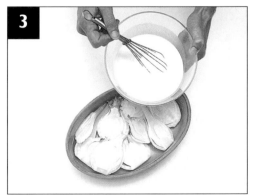

Mexican Chili Corn Pie

This bake of corn and kidney beans, flavored with chili and fresh cilantro,
is topped with crispy cheese cornbread.

Serves 4

1 tbsp corn oil
2 garlic cloves, crushed
1 red bell pepper, seeded and diced
1 green bell pepper, seeded and diced
1 celery stalk, diced
1 tsp hot chili powder
14 ounce can chopped tomatoes
11^{1}/$_{2}$ ounce can corn, drained
7^{1}/$_{2}$ ounce can kidney beans, drained and rinsed
2 tbsp chopped fresh cilantro
salt and pepper
sprigs of fresh cilantro to garnish
tomato and avocado salad, to serve

TOPPING

^{2}/$_{3}$ cup cornmeal
1 tbsp all-purpose flour
^{1}/$_{2}$ tsp salt
2 tsp baking powder
1 egg, beaten
6 tbsp milk
1 tbsp corn oil
1 cup grated sharp Cheddar

1 Heat the oil in a large skillet and gently fry the garlic, bell peppers, and celery for 5–6 minutes or until just softened.

2 Stir in the chili powder, tomatoes, sweetcorn, kidney beans, and seasoning. Bring to a boil and simmer for 10 minutes. Stir in the cilantro and spoon into an ovenproof dish.

3 To make the topping, mix together the cornmeal, flour, salt, and baking powder. Make a well in the center, add the egg, milk, and oil, and beat until a smooth batter is formed.

4 Spoon over the bell pepper and corn mixture and sprinkle with the cheese. Bake in a preheated oven at 425°F for 25–30 minutes until golden and firm.

5 Garnish with fresh cilantro sprigs and serve immediately with a tomato and avocado salad.

Cauliflower, Broccoli, & Cheese Flan

This really is a tasty flan, the pastry case for which may
be made in advance and frozen until required.

Serves 8
PASTRY
1 1/4 cups all-purpose flour
pinch of salt
1/2 tsp paprika
1 tsp dried thyme
6 tbsp vegetarian margarine
3 tbsp water
FILLING
3 1/2 ounces cauliflower florets
3 1/2 ounces broccoli florets
1 onion, cut into eight
2 tbsp butter or vegetarian margarine
1 tbsp all-purpose flour
6 tbsp vegetable stock
8 tbsp milk
3/4 cup vegetarian Cheddar cheese, grated
salt and pepper
paprika and thyme, to garnish

1 To make the pastry, sieve the flour
and salt into a bowl. Add the paprika
and thyme and rub the margarine
into the mixture until it resembles
bread crumbs. Stir in the water and
bring together to form a dough.

2 Roll the pastry out on a floured
surface and use to line a 7 inch loose-
bottomed flan pan. Prick the base
with a fork and line with baking
parchment. Fill with ceramic baking
beans and bake blind in a preheated
oven at 375°F for 15 minutes. Remove
the parchment and beans and return
the pastry case to the oven for
5 minutes.

3 To make the filling, cook the
cauliflower, broccoli, and onion in a
pan of boiling water for 10–12 minutes
until tender. Drain and reserve.

4 Melt the butter in a pan. Add the
flour and cook, stirring, for 1 minute.
Remove from the heat, stir in the
stock and milk, and return to the heat.

Bring to a boil, stirring, and add 1/2 cup
of the cheese. Season.

5 Spoon the cauliflower, broccoli, and
onion into the pastry case. Pour over
the sauce and sprinkle with the cheese.
Return to the oven for 10 minutes until
the cheese is bubbling. Dust with
paprika and garnish with thyme. Serve.

Vegetable Jalousie

This is a really easy dish to make, but looks impressive.
The mixture of vegetables gives the dish a wonderful color and flavor.

Serves 4
1 pound prepared puff pastry
1 egg, beaten
FILLING
2 tbsp butter or vegetarian margarine
1 leek, shredded
2 garlic cloves, crushed
1 red bell pepper, sliced
1 yellow bell pepper, sliced
1³/₄ ounces mushrooms sliced
2³/₄ ounces small asparagus spears
2 tbsp flour
6 tbsp vegetable stock
6 tbsp milk
4 tbsp dry white wine
1 tbsp chopped oregano
salt and pepper

1 Melt the butter or margarine in a saucepan and sauté the leek and garlic for 2 minutes, stirring. Add the remaining vegetables and cook, stirring, for 3–4 minutes.

2 Add the flour and cook for 1 minute. Remove the pan from the heat and stir in the stock, milk, and wine. Return the pan to the heat and bring to a boil, stirring, until thickened. Stir in the oregano and season with salt and pepper to taste.

3 Roll half of the pastry out on a floured surface to form a rectangle 15 inches × 6 inches. Roll out the other half of the pastry to the same shape, but a little larger. Put the smaller rectangle on a cookie sheet lined with dampened baking parchment.

4 Spoon the filling on top of the smaller rectangle, leaving a ¹/₂ inch clean edge.

5 Cut parallel slits across the larger rectangle to within 1 inch of each edge.

6 Brush the edge of the smaller rectangle with egg and place the

larger rectangle on top, sealing the edges well.

7 Brush the whole jalousie with egg and cook in a preheated oven at 400°F for 30–35 minutes until risen and golden. Serve immediately.

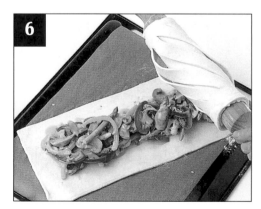

Spinach Pancake Layer

Nutty-tasting buckwheat pancakes are combined with a cheesy spinach mixture and baked with a crispy topping.

Serves 4
1 cup buckwheat flour
1 egg, beaten
1 tbsp walnut oil
1¼ cups milk
2 tsp vegetable oil
FILLING
2 pounds 4 ounces baby spinach leaves
2 tbsp water
1 bunch scallions, white and green parts, chopped
2 tsp walnut oil
1 egg, beaten
1 egg yolk
1 cup cottage cheese
½ tsp grated nutmeg
¼ cup grated Cheddar cheese
¼ cup walnut pieces
salt and pepper

1 Sift the flour into a bowl and add any husks that remain behind in the strainer. Make a well in the center and add the egg and walnut oil. Whisk in the milk to make a smooth batter. Leave to stand for 30 minutes.

2 To make the filling, wash the spinach and pack into a pan with the water. Cover tightly and cook on a high heat for 5–6 minutes until soft. Drain well and leave to cool. Fry the scallions in the walnut oil for 2–3 minutes until just soft. Drain and set aside.

3 Whisk the batter. Brush a crêpe pan with vegetable oil, heat until hot, and pour in enough batter to lightly cover the base. Cook for 1–2 minutes until set, turn, and cook for 1 minute until golden. Repeat to make 8–10 pancakes, layering them with parchment. Chop the spinach and pat dry with paper towels. Mix with the scallions, beaten egg, egg yolk, cottage cheese, nutmeg, and seasoning.

4 Layer the spinach mixture between the pancakes on a cookie sheet lined with baking parchment, finishing with a pancake on top. Sprinkle with Cheddar cheese. Bake in a preheated oven at 375°F for 20–25 minutes until firm and golden. Sprinkle with the walnuts and serve.

Cauliflower Bake

The red of the tomatoes is a great contrast to the cauliflower and herbs,
making this dish appealing to both the eye and the palate.

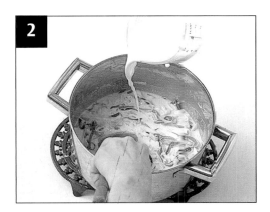

Serves 4
1 pound cauliflower, broken into florets
2 large potatoes, cubed
3½ ounces cherry tomatoes

SAUCE
2 tbsp butter or vegetarian margarine
1 leek, sliced
1 garlic clove, crushed
3 tbsp all-purpose flour
1¼ cups milk
¾ cup mixed grated cheese, such as Cheddar, Parmesan, and Gruyère
½ tsp paprika
2 tbsp chopped flat-leaf parsley
salt and pepper
chopped fresh parsley, to garnish

4 Cook in a preheated oven at 350°F for 20 minutes or until the vegetables are cooked through and the cheese is golden brown and bubbling. Garnish with fresh parsley and serve immediately.

COOK'S VARIATION

This dish could be made with broccoli instead of the cauliflower as an alternative.

1 Cook the cauliflower in a saucepan of boiling water for 10 minutes. Drain well and reserve. Meanwhile, cook the potatoes in a pan of boiling water for 10 minutes, drain, and reserve.

2 To make the sauce, melt the butter or margarine in a pan and sauté the leek and garlic for 1 minute. Add the flour and cook for 1 minute. Remove the pan from the heat and gradually stir in the milk, ½ cup of the cheese, the paprika, and parsley. Return the pan to the heat and bring to a boil, stirring. Season.

3 Spoon the cauliflower into a deep ovenproof dish. Add the cherry tomatoes and top with the potatoes. Pour the sauce over the potatoes and sprinkle on the remaining cheese.

Root Croustades with Sunshine Bell Peppers

This colorful combination of grated root vegetables and mixed bell peppers would make a stunning dinner-party dish.

Serves 4
1 orange bell pepper
1 red bell pepper
1 yellow bell pepper
3 tbsp olive oil
2 tbsp red wine vinegar
1 tsp French mustard
1 tsp clear honey
salt and pepper
sprigs of fresh flat-leaf parsley, to garnish
green vegetables, to serve

CROUSTADES

9 ounces potatoes, grated
9 ounces carrots, grated
12 ounces celery root, grated
1 garlic clove, crushed
1 tbsp lemon juice
2 tbsp butter or vegetarian margarine, melted
1 egg, beaten
1 tbsp vegetable oil

1 Place the bell peppers on a cookie sheet. Bake in a preheated oven at 375°F for 35 minutes, turning after 20 minutes. Remove the bell peppers from the oven, cover with a dish cloth, and let cool for 10 minutes. Peel the skin from the cooked bell peppers, cut in half, and discard the seeds. Thinly slice the flesh into strips and place in a shallow dish.

2 Put the oil, vinegar, mustard, honey, and seasoning in a screw-top jar and shake to mix. Pour over the bell pepper strips, toss to mix, and leave to marinate for 2 hours.

3 To make the croustades, mix the potatoes, carrots, and celery root; toss in the garlic and lemon juice. Mix in the butter or margarine and the egg. Season. Divide the mixture into 8 and pile onto 2 cookie sheets lined with baking parchment, forming each into a 4 inch round. Brush with oil. Bake in a preheated oven at 425°F for 30–35 minutes until crisp and golden. Heat the bell peppers and the marinade for 2–3 minutes, then spoon over the croustades, garnish, and serve.

Leek & Herb Soufflé

Hot soufflés look very impressive if served as soon as they
come out of the oven, otherwise they will sink quite quickly.

Serves 4
12 ounces baby leeks
1 tbsp olive oil
1/2 cup vegetable stock
1/2 cup walnuts
2 eggs, separated
2 tbsp chopped mixed herbs
2 tbsp natural yogurt
salt and pepper

1 Using a sharp knife, chop the leeks finely.

2 Heat the oil in a skillet and sauté the leeks for 2–3 minutes.

3 Add the stock to the pan and cook over a gentle heat for a further 5 minutes.

4 Place the walnuts in a food processor and blend until finely chopped.

5 Add the leek mixture to the nuts and blend to form a purée. Transfer the leek purée to a large mixing bowl.

6 Mix the egg yolks, herbs, and yogurt together and pour into the bowl containing the leek purée. Season with salt and pepper to taste and mix well.

7 In a separate mixing bowl, whisk the egg whites until they form firm peaks.

8 Using a metal spoon, fold the egg whites into the leek mixture. Spoon

the mixture into a lightly greased 1 1/2 pint ramekin dish and place on a warmed cookie sheet.

9 Cook in a preheated oven at 350°F for 35–40 minutes or until set. Serve the soufflé immediately.

COOK'S TIP

Placing the ramekin onto a warm cookie sheet helps to cook the soufflé from the bottom, thus aiding its cooking.

Spicy Stuffed Chinese Cabbage

Mushrooms, scallions, celery, and rice are flavored
with five-spice powder and wrapped in Chinese cabbage.

Serves 4
8 large Chinese cabbage leaves
$^1/_3$ cup long-grain rice
$^1/_2$ vegetable bouillon cube
$^1/_4$ cup butter
1 bunch scallions, trimmed and chopped finely
1 celery stalk, chopped finely
$4^1/_2$ ounces button mushrooms, sliced
1 tsp Chinese five-spice powder
$1^1/_4$ cups sieved tomatoes
salt and pepper
fresh chives, to garnish

1 Blanch the Chinese cabbage in a saucepan of boiling water for about 1 minute. Refresh under cold running water and drain well. Be careful not to tear the leaves.

2 Cook the rice in a saucepan of boiling water, with the bouillon cube, for 15–20 minutes or until just tender. Drain well.

3 Meanwhile, melt the butter in a skillet and fry the scallions and celery gently for 3–4 minutes until softened, but not browned. Add the mushrooms and cook for a further 3–4 minutes, stirring frequently.

4 Add the cooked rice and Chinese five-spice powder to the skillet. Season with salt and pepper to taste and stir well to combine the ingredients.

5 Lay out the Chinese leaves on a chopping board and divide the rice mixture between them. Roll each leaf into a neat packet to enclose the stuffing. making sure there are no gaps for the stuffing to escape. Place the Chinese cabbage, seam-side down, in a greased ovenproof dish.

6 Pour the sieved tomatoes over them and cover with foil.

7 Bake in a preheated oven at 375°F for 25–30 minutes. Serve immediately, garnished with fresh chives.

Artichoke & Cheese Flan

Artichoke hearts are delicious to eat, being very delicate in flavor and appearance.
They are ideal for cooking in a cheese-flavored pastry case.

Serves 8
1¼ cups whole wheat flour
2 garlic cloves, crushed
6 tbsp butter or vegetarian margarine
salt and pepper
FILLING
2 tbsp olive oil
1 red onion, halved and sliced
10 canned or fresh artichoke hearts
1 cup vegetarian Cheddar, grated
½ cup Gorgonzola cheese, crumbled
2 eggs, beaten
1 tbsp chopped fresh rosemary
⅔ cup milk

5 Spoon the artichoke and cheese mixture into the pastry case and cook in a preheated oven at 400°F for 25 minutes or until cooked and set. Serve the flan hot or cold.

COOK'S TIP

Gently press the center of the flan with your fingertip to test if it is cooked through. It should feel fairly firm, but not solid. If overcooked the flan will begin to "weep."

1 To make the pastry, sieve the flour into a mixing bowl, add a pinch of salt and the garlic. Rub in the butter or margarine until the mixture resembles bread crumbs. Stir in 3 tablespoons of water and bring the mixture together to form a dough.

2 Roll the pastry out on a lightly floured surface to fit an 8 inch flan pan. Prick the pastry with a fork.

3 Heat the oil in a skillet and sauté the onion for 3 minutes. Add the artichoke hearts and cook for a further 2 minutes.

4 Mix the cheeses with the beaten eggs, rosemary, and milk. Stir in the drained artichoke mixture and season with salt and pepper to taste.

Mushroom & Spinach Puff Pastry Packets

These puff pastry packets are easy to make and delicious to eat. Filled with garlic, mushrooms, and spinach they are ideal with a fresh tomato or cheese sauce.

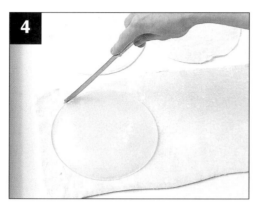

Serves 4
2 tbsp butter
1 red onion, halved and sliced
2 garlic cloves, crushed
8 ounces open-cap mushrooms, sliced
6 ounces baby spinach
pinch of nutmeg
4 tbsp heavy cream
8 ounces prepared puff pastry
1 egg, beaten
salt and pepper
2 tsp poppy seeds

1 Melt the butter in a skillet. Add the onion and garlic to the pan and sauté for 3–4 minutes, stirring well.

2 Add the mushrooms, spinach, and nutmeg and cook for a further 2–3 minutes.

3 Stir in the cream, mixing well. Season with salt and pepper to taste and remove the pan from the heat.

4 Roll the pastry out on a lightly floured surface and cut into four 6 inch circles.

5 Spoon a quarter of the filling onto one half of each circle and fold the pastry over to encase the filling. Seal the edges of the pastry and brush with the beaten egg. Sprinkle with the poppy seeds.

6 Place the packets onto a dampened cookie sheet and cook in a preheated oven at 400°F for 20 minutes until risen and golden brown.

7 Transfer the mushroom and spinach puff pastry packets to serving plates and serve immediately.

COOK'S TIP

The cookie sheet is dampened so that steam forms with the heat of the oven and helps the pastry to rise and set.

Vegetable & Bean Curd Strudels

These strudels look really impressive and are perfect if friends are coming round or for a more formal dinner party dish.

Serves 4
FILLING
2 tbsp vegetable oil
2 tbsp butter or vegetarian margarine
5^1/$_2$ ounces potatoes finely diced
1 leek, shredded
2 garlic cloves, crushed
1 tsp garam masala
^{1}/$_2$ tsp chili powder
^{1}/$_2$ tsp turmeric
1^3/$_4$ ounces okra, sliced
3^1/$_2$ ounces button mushrooms, sliced
2 tomatoes, diced
8 ounces firm bean curd, diced
12 sheets filo pastry
2 tbsp butter or vegetarian margarine, melted
salt and pepper

1 To make the filling, heat the oil and butter in a skillet. Add the potatoes and leek and cook for 2–3 minutes, stirring.

2 Add the garlic, spices, okra, mushrooms, tomatoes, bean curd, and seasoning and cook, stirring, for 5–7 minutes or until tender.

3 Lay the pastry out on a chopping board and brush each individual sheet with butter. Place 3 sheets on top of one another; repeat to make 4 stacks.

4 Spoon a quarter of the filling along the center of each stack and brush the edges with butter. Fold the short edges in and roll up lengthwise to form a cigar shape;

brush the outside with butter. Place the strudels on a greased cookie sheet.

5 Cook in a preheated oven at 375°F and cook the strudels for 20 minutes or until golden brown. Serve immediately.

COOK'S TIP

Decorate the outside of the strudels with crumpled pastry trimmings before cooking for a really impressive effect.

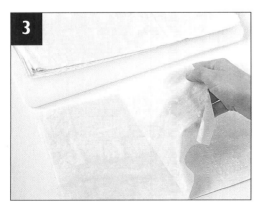

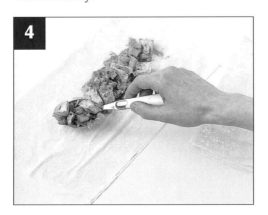

Vegetable Toad-in-the-Hole

This dish can be made in one large dish or in
individual Yorkshire pudding pans.

Serves 4
BATTER
³/₄ cup all-purpose flour
2 eggs, beaten
³/₄ cup milk
2 tbsp wholegrain mustard
2 tbsp vegetable oil
FILLING
2 tbsp butter
2 garlic cloves, crushed
1 onion, cut into eight
2³/₄ ounces baby carrots, halved lengthwise
1³/₄ ounces green beans
1³/₄ ounces canned corn, drained
2 tomatoes, seeded and cut into chunks
1 tsp wholegrain mustard
1 tbsp chopped mixed herbs
salt and pepper

1 To make the batter, sieve the
flour and a pinch of salt into a large
bowl. Make a well in the center and
beat in the eggs and milk to make a
batter. Stir in the mustard and leave
to stand.

2 Pour the vegetable oil into a
shallow ovenproof dish and heat in
a preheated oven at 400°F for
10 minutes.

3 Meanwhile, make the filling. Melt
the butter in a skillet and sauté the
garlic and onion for 2 minutes,
stirring. Cook the carrots and beans in
a saucepan of boiling water for
7 minutes or until tender. Drain well.

4 Add the corn and tomato to the
skillet with the mustard and herbs.
Season well and add the carrots
and beans.

5 Remove the dish from the oven
and pour in the batter. Spoon the
vegetables into the center, return to
the oven, and cook for 30–35 minutes
until the batter has risen and set.

6 Serve the vegetable toad-in-the-hole
immediately.

COOK'S TIP

It is important that the oil is hot
before adding the batter so that
the batter begins to cook and
rise immediately.

Almond & Sesame Nut Roast

Toasted almonds are combined with sesame seeds, rice, and vegetables in this
tasty vegetarian roast. Serve with a delicious onion and mushroom sauce.

Serves 4
2 tbsp sesame or olive oil
1 small onion, chopped finely
scant ¹/₄ cup risotto rice
1¹/₄ cups Fresh Vegetable Stock (see page 14)
1 large carrot, grated
1 large leek, trimmed and chopped finely
2 tsp sesame seeds, toasted
³/₄ cup chopped almonds, toasted
¹/₂ cup ground almonds
³/₄ cup sharp Cheddar, grated
2 eggs, beaten
1 tsp dried mixed herbs
salt and pepper
sprigs of flat-leaf parsley, to garnish
fresh vegetables, to serve

SAUCE
2 tbsp butter
1 small onion, chopped finely
4¹/₂ ounces mushrooms, chopped finely
¹/₄ cup all-purpose flour
1¹/₄ cups Fresh Vegetable Stock (see page 14)

1 Heat the oil in a skillet and fry the
onion gently for 2–3 minutes. Add the
rice and cook gently for 5–6 minutes,
stirring frequently.

2 Add the vegetable stock, bring to a
boil, and then simmer for about
15 minutes, or until the rice is tender.
Add a little extra water if necessary.
Remove the pan from the heat and
transfer the rice to a large bowl.

3 Add the carrot, leek, sesame seeds,
almonds, cheese, beaten eggs, and
herbs to the mixture. Mix well and
season. Transfer the mixture to a
greased 1 pound 2 ounce loaf pan,
levelling the surface. Bake in a
preheated oven at 350°F for about
1 hour, or until set and firm. Leave
in the pan for 10 minutes.

4 To make the sauce, melt the butter
in a small saucepan and fry the onion

until dark golden brown. Add the
mushrooms and cook for a further
2 minutes. Stir in the flour, cook
gently for 1 minute, and then
gradually add the stock. Bring to a boil,
stirring constantly, until thickened
and blended. Season to taste.

5 Turn out the nut roast, slice, and
serve on warmed plates with fresh
vegetables, accompanied by the sauce.
Garnish with sprigs of flat-leaf parsley.

Green Vegetable Gougère

A tasty, simple supper dish of choux pastry and crisp green vegetables.
You can vary the vegetables according to taste.

Serves 4
1¹/₄ cups all-purpose flour
¹/₂ cup butter or vegetarian margarine
1¹/₄ cups water
4 eggs, beaten
³/₄ cup grated Gruyère cheese
1 tbsp milk
salt and pepper

FILLING
2 tbsp garlic and herb butter or margarine
2 tsp olive oil
2 leeks, shredded
9 ounces green cabbage, shredded finely
4¹/₂ ounces bean sprouts
¹/₂ tsp grated lime rind
1 tbsp lime juice
celery salt and pepper
lime slices, to garnish

1 Sift the flour onto a piece of baking parchment and set aside. Cut the butter or margarine into dice and put in a saucepan with the water. Heat until the butter has melted.

2 Bring the butter and water to a boil, then using the baking parchment as a funnel, shoot in the flour all at once. Beat until the mixture becomes thick. Remove from the heat and beat until the mixture is glossy and comes away from the sides of the saucepan.

3 Transfer to a bowl and cool for 10 minutes. Beat in the eggs, a little at a time, ensuring they are incorporated after each addition. Stir in ¹/₂ cup of the cheese and season with salt and pepper to taste.

4 Dampen a cookie sheet. Place spoonfuls of the mixture in a 9 inch circle on the cookie sheet. Brush with milk and sprinkle with the remaining cheese. Bake in a preheated oven at 425°F for 30–35 minutes until golden and crisp. Transfer to a serving plate.

5 Make the filling about 5 minutes before the end of cooking time. Heat the garlic butter or margarine and the oil in a skillet and stir-fry the leeks and cabbage for 2 minutes.

6 Add the bean sprouts, lime rind, and juice and cook for 1 minute, stirring. Season with celery salt and pepper to taste, then pile into the center of the cooked pastry ring. Garnish with lime slices and serve.

Filled Jacket Potatoes

Cook these potatoes conventionally, wrap them in foil, and keep warm
at the edge of the barbecue, ready to fill with inspired mixtures.

Serves 4

4 large or 8 medium baking potatoes

paprika or chili powder, or chopped
fresh herbs, to garnish

MEXICAN CORN RELISH

9 ounce can corn, drained

$1/2$ red bell pepper, seeded
and chopped finely

2 inch piece cucumber,
chopped finely

$1/2$ tsp chili powder

salt and pepper

BLUE CHEESE, CELERY, & CHIVE FILLING

$1/2$ cup full-fat soft cheese

$1/2$ cup natural fromage frais

$4^{1}/2$ ounces blue cheese, cut into cubes

1 celery stalk, chopped finely

2 tsp snipped fresh chives

celery salt and pepper

MUSHROOMS IN SPICY TOMATO SAUCE

2 tbsp butter or vegetarian margarine

9 ounces button mushrooms

$2/3$ cup natural yogurt

1 tbsp tomato paste

2 tsp mild curry powder

salt and pepper

1 Scrub the potatoes and prick them with a fork. Bake in a preheated oven at 400°F for about 1 hour, or until just tender.

2 To make the Mexican Corn Relish, put half of the corn into a bowl. Put the remainder into a blender or food processor for 10–15 seconds, or chop and mash roughly by hand. Add the puréed corn to the corn kernels with the bell pepper, cucumber, and chili powder. Season with salt and pepper to taste.

3 To make the Blue Cheese, Celery, & Chive Filling, mix the soft cheese and fromage frais together until smooth. Add the blue cheese, celery, and chives and mix until well combined. Season to taste with celery salt and pepper.

4 To make the Mushrooms in Spicy Tomato Sauce, melt the butter or margarine in a small skillet. Add the mushrooms and cook gently for 3–4 minutes. Remove from the heat and stir in the yogurt, tomato paste, and curry powder. Season.

5 Wrap the cooked potatoes in foil and keep warm at the edge of the barbecue. Serve the fillings sprinkled with paprika or chili powder or herbs.

Side Dishes
& Salads

An ideal accompaniment complements the main dish both visually and nutritionally. Many of the main dishes contained in this book will be rich in protein, therefore the side dishes in this chapter have been designed to be a little lighter in texture, while containing other important nutrients and lots of flavor and color. The recipes contained within this chapter are perfect

accompaniments for all occasions. A salad also makes a refreshing accompaniment to the main course. You could even

serve two or three salads together as a complete meal—they are a good source of vitamins and minerals. Always use the freshest possible ingredients for maximum flavor and texture.

Pepperonata

A delicious mixture of bell peppers and onions, cooked
with tomatoes and herbs for a rich side dish.

Serves 4
4 tbsp olive oil
1 onion, halved and finely sliced
2 red bell peppers, cut into strips
2 green bell peppers, cut into strips
2 yellow bell peppers, cut into strips
2 garlic cloves, crushed
2 x 14 ounce cans chopped tomatoes, drained
2 tbsp chopped cilantro
2 tbsp chopped pitted black olives
salt and pepper

1 Heat the oil in a large skillet. Add the onion and sauté for 5 minutes, stirring until just beginning to color.

2 Add the bell peppers and garlic to the pan and cook for a further 3–4 minutes. Stir in the tomatoes and cilantro and season well. Cover the pan and cook the vegetables gently for about 30 minutes or until the mixture is dry.

3 Stir in the olives and serve immediately.

COOK'S TIP

Stir the vegetables occasionally during the 30 minutes cooking time to prevent them sticking to the bottom of the pan. If the liquid has not evaporated by the end of the cooking time, remove the lid, and boil rapidly until the dish is dry.

Cheese & Potato Layer Bake

This really is a great side dish, perfect for serving
with main meals cooked in the oven.

Serves 4
1 pound potatoes
1 leek, sliced
3 garlic cloves, crushed
1/2 cup Cheddar, grated
1/2 cup Mozzarella, grated
1/4 cup Parmesan cheese grated
2 tbsp chopped parsley
2/3 cup light cream
2/3 cup milk
salt and pepper
freshly chopped flat-leaf parsley to garnish

1 Cook the potatoes in a saucepan of boiling, salted water for 10 minutes. Drain well. Cut the potatoes into thin slices. Arrange a layer of potatoes in the base of an ovenproof dish. Layer with a little of the leek, garlic, cheese, and parsley. Season well.

2 Repeat the layers until all of the ingredients have been used, finishing with a layer of cheese on top.

3 Mix the cream and milk together, season, and pour over the potato layers. Cook in a preheated oven at 325°F for 1–1¼ hours or until golden brown and bubbling and the potatoes are cooked through. Garnish and serve.

COOK'S TIP

Prepare the dish in advance, cover, and chill for up to 12 hours until required.

Greek Green Beans

This dish contains many Greek flavors such as lemon, garlic, oregano, and olives, for a really flavorful recipe.

Serves 4
14 ounce can navy beans, drained
1 tbsp olive oil
3 garlic cloves, crushed
2 cups vegetable stock
1 bay leaf
2 sprigs oregano
1 tbsp tomato paste
juice of 1 lemon
1 small red onion, chopped
1 ounce pitted black olives, halved
salt and pepper

1 Put the navy beans in a flameproof casserole dish.

2 Add the olive oil and garlic and cook over a gentle heat, stirring occasionally, for 4–5 minutes.

3 Add the stock, bay leaf, oregano, tomato paste, lemon juice, and red onion, cover, and simmer for about 1 hour or until the sauce has thickened.

4 Stir in the olives, season with salt and pepper to taste, and serve.

COOK'S TIP

This dish may be made in advance and served cold with crusty bread, if preferred.

Cauliflower & Broccoli with Herb Sauce

Whole baby cauliflowers are used in this recipe. Try to find them if you can, if not use large bunches of florets.

Serves 4
2 baby cauliflowers
8 ounces broccoli
salt and pepper
SAUCE
8 tbsp olive oil
4 tbsp butter or vegetarian margarine
2 tsp grated root ginger
juice and rind of 2 lemons
5 tbsp chopped cilantro
5 tbsp grated Cheddar

1 Cut the cauliflowers in half and the broccoli into very large florets. Cook the cauliflower and broccoli in a saucepan of boiling, salted water for 10 minutes. Drain well and transfer to a shallow ovenproof dish.

2 To make the sauce, put the oil and butter or margarine in a pan and heat gently until the butter melts. Add the ginger, lemon juice and rind, and cilantro and simmer for 2–3 minutes.

3 Pour the sauce over the vegetables in the dish and sprinkle the cheese on top. Cook under a hot broiler for 2–3 minutes or until the cheese is bubbling and serve immediately.

COOK'S VARIATION

Lime or orange could be used instead of the lemon for a fruity and refreshing sauce.

Pesto Potatoes

Pesto sauce is more commonly used as a pasta sauce but it is delicious served over potatoes as well.

Serves 4
2 pounds small new potatoes
2³/₄ ounces fresh basil
2 tbsp pine nuts
3 garlic cloves, crushed
¹/₂ cup olive oil
³/₄ cup freshly grated Parmesan cheese and Pecorino cheese, mixed
salt and pepper
fresh basil sprigs, to garnish

1 Cook the potatoes in a saucepan of boiling, salted water for 15 minutes or until tender. Drain well, transfer to a warm serving dish, and keep warm.

2 Meanwhile, put the basil, pine nuts, garlic, and a little salt and pepper to taste in a food processor. Blend for 30 seconds, adding the oil gradually, until smooth.

3 Remove the mixture from the food processor and stir in the cheeses.

4 Spoon the pesto sauce over the potatoes and mix well. Garnish with fresh basil sprigs and serve immediately.

COOK'S TIP

This sauce would also make a great salad dressing for a crisp green salad.

Sweet & Sour Eggplants

This is a dish of Persian origin, not Chinese as it sounds. Eggplants are fried and mixed with tomatoes, mint, sugar, and vinegar for a really intense flavor.

Serves 4
2 large eggplants, cubed
6 tbsp olive oil
4 garlic cloves, crushed
1 onion, cut into eight
4 large tomatoes, seeded and chopped
3 tbsp chopped mint
4 tsp brown sugar
2 tbsp red wine vinegar
1 tsp chili flakes
salt and pepper
fresh mint sprigs, to garnish

1 Put the eggplants in a colander, sprinkle with salt, and leave to stand for 30 minutes. Rinse under cold running water and drain well. Pat dry with absorbent paper towels.

2 Heat the oil in a large skillet and sauté the eggplants, stirring constantly, for 1–2 minutes.

3 Stir in the garlic and onion and cook for a further 2–3 minutes.

4 Stir in the tomatoes, mint, and stock, cover, and cook for 15–20 minutes or until the vegetables are tender.

5 Stir in the sugar, vinegar, and chili, season with salt and pepper to taste, and cook for 2–3 minutes. Garnish with fresh mint sprigs and serve.

Spicy Lentils & Spinach

This is quite a filling dish, and should be served with a light main course.
Green split peas are a type of lentil.

Serves 4
1¼ cups green split peas
2 pounds spinach
4 tbsp vegetable oil
1 onion, halved and sliced
1 tsp grated root ginger
1 tsp ground cumin
½ tsp chili powder
½ tsp ground coriander
2 garlic cloves, crushed
1¼ cups vegetable stock
salt and pepper
fresh cilantro sprigs and lime wedges, to garnish

1 Rinse the peas under cold running water. Transfer to a mixing bowl, cover with cold water, and leave to soak for 2 hours. Drain well.

2 Meanwhile, cook the spinach in a large saucepan for 5 minutes until wilted. Drain well and roughly chop.

3 Heat the oil in a large saucepan and sauté the onion, spices, and garlic for 2–3 minutes, stirring well.

4 Add the peas and spinach and stir in the stock. Cover and simmer for 10–15 minutes or until the peas are cooked and the liquid has been absorbed. Season, garnish, and serve.

COOK'S TIP

Once the peas have been added, stir occasionally to prevent them from sticking to the pan.

Mini Vegetable Puff Pastry Cases

These are ideal with a more formal meal as they take
a little time to prepare and look really impressive.

Serves 4
1 pound puff pastry
1 egg, beaten

FILLING

8 ounces sweet potato, cubed
3$^{1}/_{2}$ ounces baby asparagus spears
2 tbsp butter or vegetarian margarine
1 leek, sliced
2 small open-cap mushrooms, sliced
1 tsp lime juice
1 tsp chopped thyme
pinch of dried mustard
salt and pepper

1 Cut the pastry into 4 equal pieces. Roll each piece out on a lightly floured surface to form a 5 inch square. Place on a dampened cookie sheet and score a smaller 2.5 inch square inside. Brush with beaten egg and cook in a preheated oven at 400°F for 20 minutes or until risen and golden brown.

2 Remove from the oven, then carefully cut out the central square of pastry, lift out, and reserve.

3 To make the filling, cook the sweet potato in a saucepan of boiling water for 15 minutes, then drain well. Blanch the asparagus in a saucepan of boiling water for 10 minutes or until tender. Drain and reserve.

4 Melt the butter or vegetarian margarine in a saucepan and sauté the leek and mushrooms for 2–3 minutes. Add the lime juice, thyme, and mustard, season well, and stir in the sweet potatoes and asparagus. Spoon into the pastry cases, top with the reserved pastry squares, and serve immediately.

COOK'S TIP

Use a colorful selection of any vegetables you have to hand for this recipe.

Steamed Vegetables with Vermouth

Serve these vegetables in their paper packets to retain the juices.
The result is truly delicious.

Serves 4
1 carrot, cut into batons
1 fennel bulb, sliced
3½ ounces zucchini, sliced
1 red bell pepper, sliced
4 small onions, halved
8 tbsp vermouth
4 tbsp lime juice
zest of 1 lime
pinch of paprika
4 sprigs tarragon
salt and pepper
fresh tarragon sprigs, to garnish

1 Place all of the vegetables in a large bowl and mix well.

2 Cut 4 large squares of greaseproof paper and place a quarter of the vegetables in the center of each. Bring the sides of the paper up and pinch together to make an open packet.

3 Mix the vermouth, lime juice, lime zest, and paprika and pour a quarter of the mixture into each packet. Season and add a tarragon sprig to each. Pinch the tops of the packets together to seal.

4 Place the vegetable parcels in a steamer, cover, and cook for 15–20 minutes or until the vegetables are tender. Garnish and serve.

COOK'S TIP

Seal the packets well to prevent them opening during cooking and causing the juices to evaporate.

Curried Cauliflower & Spinach

The contrast in color in this recipe makes it very appealing to the eye, especially as the cauliflower is lightly colored with yellow turmeric.

Serves 4
1 medium cauliflower
6 tbsp vegetable oil
1 tsp mustard seeds
1 tsp ground cumin
1 tsp garam masala
1 tsp turmeric
2 garlic cloves, crushed
1 onion, halved and sliced
1 green chili, sliced
1 pound spinach
6 tbsp vegetable stock
1 tbsp chopped cilantro
salt and pepper
cilantro sprigs, to garnish

1 Break the cauliflower into small florets.

2 Heat the oil in a deep flameproof casserole dish. Add the mustard seeds and cook until they begin to pop. Stir in the remaining spices, the garlic, onion, and chili and cook for 2–3 minutes, stirring.

3 Add the cauliflower, spinach, stock, cilantro, and seasoning, cover, and cook over a gentle heat for 15 minutes or until the cauliflower is tender. Uncover the dish and boil for 1 minute to thicken the juices. Garnish with fresh cilantro and serve.

COOK'S VARIATION

Broccoli may be used instead of the cauliflower, if preferred.

Soufflèd Cheesy Potato Fries

These small potato chunks are mixed in a creamy cheese sauce and
fried in oil until deliciously golden brown.

Serves 4
2 pounds potatoes, cut into chunks
$^2/_3$ cup heavy cream
$^3/_4$ cup Gruyère cheese, grated
pinch of cayenne pepper
2 egg whites
oil, for deep-frying
salt and pepper
chopped flat-leaf parsley and grated vegetarian cheese, to garnish

1 Cook the potatoes in a saucepan of boiling, salted water for 10 minutes. Drain well and pat dry with absorbent paper towels.

2 Mix the cream and cheese in a large bowl. Stir in the cayenne pepper and season to taste.

3 Whisk the egg whites until stiff peaks form. Fold into the cheese mixture until fully incorporated. Add the potatoes, turning to coat.

4 Heat the oil for deep-frying to 350°F or until a cube of bread browns in 30 seconds. Remove the potatoes from the cheese mixture with a slotted spoon and cook in the oil, in batches, for 3–4 minutes or until golden. Transfer to a serving dish, garnish, and serve.

COOK'S VARIATION

Add other flavorings, such as grated nutmeg or curry powder, to the cream and cheese.

Baked Celery with Cream & Pecans

This dish is topped with bread crumbs for a crunchy topping, underneath
which is hidden a creamy celery and pecan mixture.

Serves 4
1 head of celery
¹/₂ tsp ground cumin
¹/₂ tsp ground coriander
1 garlic clove, crushed
1 red onion, thinly sliced
¹/₂ cup pecan nut halves
²/₃ cup vegetable stock
²/₃ cup light cream
1³/₄ ounces fresh whole wheat bread crumbs
¹/₄ cup Parmesan cheese, grated
salt and pepper
celery leaves, to garnish

1 Trim the celery and cut into matchsticks. Place the celery in an ovenproof dish with the ground cumin, coriander, garlic, onion, and pecan nuts.

2 Mix the stock and cream together and pour over the vegetables. Season with salt and pepper to taste.

3 Mix the bread crumbs and cheese together and sprinkle over the top to cover the vegetables. Cook in a preheated oven at 400°F for 40 minutes or until the vegetables are tender and the top crispy. Garnish with celery leaves and serve at once.

COOK'S VARIATION

You could use carrots or zucchini
instead of the celery,
if you prefer.

Beans in Lemon & Herb Sauce

Use a variety of beans if possible, although this recipe is
perfectly acceptable with just one type of bean.

Serves 4
2 pounds mixed green beans, such as fava beans, green beans, runner beans
$1/2$ cup butter or vegetarian margarine
4 tsp all-purpose flour
$1^{1}/_{4}$ cups vegetable stock
$1/3$ cup dry white wine
6 tbsp light cream
3 tbsp chopped mixed herbs
2 tbsp lemon juice
zest of 1 lemon
salt and pepper

1 Cook the beans in a saucepan of boiling, salted water for 10 minutes or until tender. Drain and place in a warm serving dish.

2 Meanwhile, melt the butter in a saucepan. Add the flour and cook for 1 minute. Remove the pan from the heat and gradually stir in the stock and wine. Return the pan to the heat and bring to a boil.

3 Remove the pan from the heat once again and stir in the cream, herbs, lemon juice, and rind. Season to taste. Pour the sauce over the beans, mixing well. Serve.

COOK'S TIP

Use a wide variety of herbs for flavor, such as rosemary, thyme, tarragon, and sage.

Indian Spiced Potatoes & Spinach

This is a classic Indian accompaniment for
curries or plainer main vegetable dishes.

Serves 4
3 tbsp vegetable oil
1 red onion, sliced
2 garlic cloves, crushed
$^1/_2$ tsp chili powder
2 tsp ground coriander
1 tsp ground cumin
$^2/_3$ cup vegetable stock
10$^1/_2$ ounces potatoes, cubed
1 pound baby spinach
1 red chili, sliced
salt and pepper

1 Heat the oil in a skillet and sauté
the onion and garlic for 2–5 minutes,
stirring. Stir in the chili powder,
ground coriander, and cumin and
cook for a further 30 seconds.

2 Add the stock, potato, and spinach
and bring to a boil. Reduce the
heat, cover, and simmer for about
10 minutes or until the potatoes are
cooked through.

3 Uncover, season, add the chili, and
cook for a further 2–3 minutes. Serve.

COOK'S VARIATION

Add other vegetables,
such as chopped tomatoes, for color
and flavor.

Bulgar Pilau

Bulgar wheat is very easy to use and is a delicious alternative to rice, having a distinctive nutty flavor.

Serves 4

6 tbsp butter or
vegetarian margarine

1 red onion, halved and sliced

2 garlic cloves, crushed

2 cups bulgar wheat

6 ounces tomatoes, seeded
and chopped

1³/₄ ounces baby corn cobs,
halved lengthwise

2³/₄ ounces small
broccoli florets

3³/₄ cups vegetable
stock

2 tbsp clear honey

1³/₄ ounces golden raisins

1³/₄ ounces pine nuts

¹/₂ tsp ground cinnamon

¹/₂ tsp ground cumin

salt and pepper

sliced scallions,
to garnish

1 Melt the butter or margarine in a large flameproof casserole dish.

2 Add the onion and garlic and sauté for 2–3 minutes, stirring occasionally.

3 Add the bulgar wheat, tomatoes, corn cobs, broccoli, and stock and bring to a boil. Reduce the heat, cover, and cook for 15–20 minutes, stirring occasionally.

4 Stir in the honey, golden raisins, nuts, ground cinnamon, cumin, and salt and pepper to taste, mixing well. Remove the casserole from the heat, cover, and leave for 10 minutes.

5 Spoon the bulgar pilau into a warm serving dish.

6 Garnish the bulgar pilau with sliced scallions and serve immediately.

COOK'S TIP

The dish is left to stand for 10 minutes in order for the bulgar wheat to finish cooking and the flavors to mingle.

Carrot, Orange, & Poppy Seed Bake

The poppy seeds add texture and flavor to this recipe,
and counteract the slightly sweet flavor of the carrots.

Serves 4
1 pound 8 ounces carrots, cut into thin strips
1 leek, sliced
1¼ cups fresh orange juice
2 tbsp clear honey
1 garlic clove, crushed
1 tsp mixed spice
2 tsp chopped thyme
1 tbsp poppy seeds
salt and pepper
fresh thyme sprigs and orange zest, to garnish

1 Cook the carrots and leek in a saucepan of boiling, salted water for 5–6 minutes. Drain well and transfer to a shallow baking dish.

2 Mix together the orange juice, honey, garlic, mixed spice, and thyme and pour the mixture over the vegetables. Season to taste with salt and pepper.

3 Cover and cook in a preheated oven at 350°F for 30 minutes or until the vegetables are tender. Remove the lid and sprinkle with poppy seeds. Garnish and serve.

COOK'S TIP

Lemon or lime juice could be used instead of the orange juice, if you prefer. Garnish with lemon or lime zest.

Eggplant & Zucchini Galette

This is a dish of eggplants and zucchini layered with
a quick tomato sauce and melted cheese.

Serves 4
2 large eggplants, sliced
4 zucchini
2 x 14 ounce cans chopped tomatoes, drained
2 tbsp tomato paste
2 garlic cloves, crushed
4 tbsp olive oil
1 tsp superfine sugar
2 tbsp chopped basil
olive oil, for frying
8 ounces Mozzarella cheese, sliced
salt and pepper
fresh basil leaves, to garnish

1 Put the eggplant slices in a colander and sprinkle with salt. Leave to stand for 30 minutes, then rinse well under cold water, and drain. Thinly slice the zucchini.

2 Meanwhile, put the tomatoes, tomato paste, garlic, olive oil, sugar, and chopped basil into a pan and simmer for 20 minutes or until reduced by half. Season well.

3 Heat 2 tablespoons of olive oil in a large skillet and cook the eggplant slices for 2–3 minutes until just beginning to brown. Remove from the pan.

4 Add a further 2 tablespoons of oil to the pan and fry the zucchini slices until browned.

5 Arrange half of the eggplant slices in the base of an ovenproof dish.

Top with half of the tomato sauce and the zucchini and then half of the Mozzarella cheese. Repeat the layers and bake in a preheated oven at 350°F for 45–50 minutes or until the vegetables are tender. Garnish with fresh basil leaves and serve immediately.

COOK'S TIP

Add a little more oil when frying the vegetables, if required, and fry in batches to brown all of the slices evenly. The eggplant will absorb the oil quickly.

Red Onion, Cherry Tomato, & Pasta Salad

Pasta tastes perfect in this lively salad, dressed with
red wine vinegar, lemon juice, basil, and olive oil.

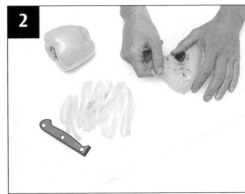

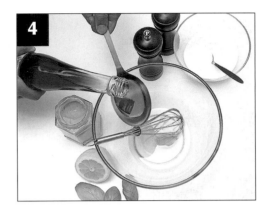

Serves 4

6 ounces pasta shapes

1 yellow bell pepper,
halved and seeded

2 small zucchini, sliced

1 red onion, sliced thinly

$4^{1}/_{2}$ ounces cherry
tomatoes, halved

salt

sprigs of fresh basil
to garnish

DRESSING

4 tbsp olive oil

2 tbsp red wine vinegar

2 tsp lemon juice

1 tsp Dijon mustard

$^{1}/_{2}$ tsp superfine sugar

handful of fresh basil leaves,
torn into small pieces

salt and pepper

1 Cook the pasta in a saucepan of
lightly salted, boiling water for about
8 minutes, or until just tender.

2 Meanwhile, place the bell pepper
halves, skin-side uppermost, under a
preheated broiler until they just begin
to char. Leave them to cool, then peel,
and slice them into strips.

3 Cook the zucchini in a small
amount of lightly salted, boiling water
for 3–4 minutes, until cooked, yet still
crunchy. Drain and refresh under cold
running water to cool quickly.

4 To make the dressing, mix together
the olive oil, red wine vinegar, lemon

juice, mustard, and sugar. Season with
salt and pepper to taste. Add the basil
leaves and mix well.

5 Drain the pasta and transfer it to a
large serving bowl. Add the dressing
and toss well. Add the bell pepper,
zucchini, onion, and cherry tomatoes,

stirring to combine. Cover and leave
at room temperature for about
30 minutes to allow the flavors
to develop.

6 Garnish the red onion, cherry
tomato, and pasta salad with sprigs of
fresh basil and serve.

Zucchini & Mint Salad

This salad uses lots of green-colored ingredients which look and taste wonderful with the minty yogurt dressing.

Serves 4
2 zucchini, cut into sticks
3½ ounces green beans, cut into three
1 green bell pepper, cut into strips
2 celery sticks, sliced
1 bunch watercress

DRESSING

¾ cup natural yogurt
1 garlic clove, crushed
2 tbsp chopped mint
pepper

1 Cook the zucchini and beans in a saucepan of salted, boiling water for 7–8 minutes. Drain and leave to cool completely.

2 Mix the vegetables with the bell pepper, celery, and watercress in a large bowl.

3 To make the dressing, mix the yogurt, garlic, mint, and pepper to taste in a bowl.

4 Spoon the dressing onto the salad and serve immediately.

COOK'S TIP

The salad must be served as soon as the yogurt dressing has been added—the dressing will separate if kept for any length of time.

Goat Cheese Salad

A delicious hot salad of melting goat cheese over sliced
tomato and basil on a base of hot ciabatta bread.

Serves 4
3 tbsp olive oil
1 tbsp white wine vinegar
1 tsp black olive paste
1 garlic clove, crushed
1 tsp chopped fresh thyme
1 ciabatta loaf
4 small tomatoes
12 fresh basil leaves
4 1/2 ounces logs goat cheese

TO SERVE

mixed salad greens, including
arugula and radicchio

1 Mix the oil, vinegar, olive paste,
garlic, and thyme together in a screw-
top jar and shake vigorously.

2 Cut the ciabatta in half horizontally,
then in half vertically to make
4 pieces.

3 Drizzle some of the dressing over
the bread, then arrange the tomatoes
and basil leaves on top.

4 Cut each roll of goat cheese into
6 slices and lay 3 slices on each piece
of ciabatta.

5 Brush with some of the dressing
and place in a preheated oven at
450°F for 5–6 minutes until just
turning brown at the edges.

6 Pour the remaining dressing over
the salad greens and serve with the
baked bread.

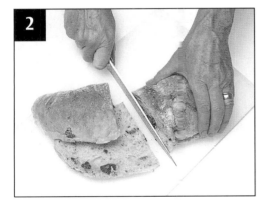

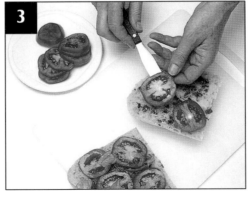

Alfalfa, Beetroot, & Spinach Salad

This is a really refreshing salad that must be assembled just before serving
to prevent all of the ingredients being tainted pink by the beetroot.

Serves 4
3½ ounces baby spinach
2¾ ounces alfalfa sprouts
2 celery sticks, sliced
4 cooked beetroot, cut into eight
DRESSING
4 tbsp olive oil
1½ tbsp garlic wine vinegar
1 garlic clove, crushed
2 tsp clear honey
1 tbsp chopped chives

1 Place the spinach and alfalfa sprouts in a large bowl and mix together.

2 Add the celery and mix well.

3 Toss in the beetroot and mix well.

4 To make the dressing, mix the oil, wine vinegar, garlic, honey, and chopped chives.

5 Pour the dressing over the salad, toss well, and serve immediately.

COOK'S TIP

Alfalfa sprouts should be available from most supermarkets, if not, use bean sprouts instead.

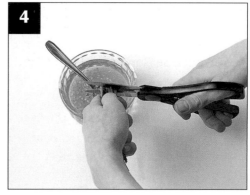

Moroccan Orange & Couscous Salad

Couscous is a type of semolina made from durum wheat. It is wonderful
in salads as it readily absorbs the flavor of the dressing.

Serves 4-6
2 cups couscous
1 bunch scallions, trimmed and chopped finely
1 small green bell pepper, seeded and chopped
4 inch piece cucumber, chopped
6 ounce can garbanzo beans, rinsed and drained
$2/3$ cup golden raisins or raisins
2 oranges
salt and pepper
mixed salad greens, to serve
sprigs of fresh mint, to garnish

DRESSING

finely grated rind of 1 orange
1 tbsp chopped fresh mint
$2/3$ cup natural yogurt

1 Place the couscous in a large bowl,
cover with boiling water, and leave to
soak for about 15 minutes or until the
grains have swelled. Stir with a fork to
separate the grains.

2 Add the scallions, green bell
pepper, cucumber, garbanzo beans,
and golden raisins or raisins to the
couscous, stirring to combine all the
ingredients. Season well with salt and
pepper to taste.

3 To make the dressing, mix the
orange rind, mint, and yogurt. Pour
over the couscous mixture and
stir well.

4 Using a sharp serrated knife,
remove the peel and pith from
the oranges.

5 Cut the orange flesh into segments,
removing all the membrane.

6 Arrange the mixed salad greens
on 4 serving plates. Divide the
couscous mixture between the plates
and arrange the orange segments on
top. Garnish with sprigs of fresh mint
and serve.

Eggplant Salad

This salad uses sesame seed paste as a flavoring
for the dressing, which complements the eggplant.

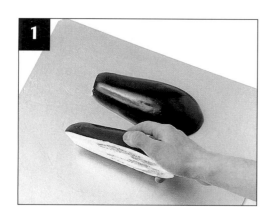  

Serves 4
1 large eggplant
3 tbsp sesame seed paste
juice and rind of 1 lemon
1 garlic clove, crushed
pinch of paprika
1 tbsp chopped cilantro
Little Gem lettuce leaves
salt and pepper

TO SERVE:

strips of pimiento
lemon wedges
toasted sesame seeds

1 Cut the eggplant in half and place,
skin-side uppermost, on an oiled
cookie sheet. Cook in a preheated
oven at 450°F for 10–15 minutes.
Remove from the oven and let cool.

2 Cut the eggplant into cubes and
reserve. Mix the sesame seed paste,
lemon juice and rind, garlic, paprika,
and cilantro together. Season and stir
in the eggplant.

3 Line a serving dish with lettuce
leaves and spoon the salad into the
center. Garnish with pimiento slices,
lemon wedges and toasted sesame
seeds, and serve.

COOK'S TIP

Sesame seed paste is available from
most health food shops.

Carrot & Cashew Nut Coleslaw

This simple salad has a dressing made from poppy seeds
pan-fried in sesame oil to bring out their flavor.

Serves 4
1 large carrot, grated
1 small onion, chopped finely
2 celery stalks, chopped
1/4 small, hard white cabbage, shredded
1 tbsp chopped fresh parsley
4 tbsp sesame oil
1/2 tsp poppy seeds
1/2 cup cashew nuts
2 tbsp white wine or cider vinegar
salt and pepper
chopped parsley, to garnish

1 In a large salad bowl, mix together
the carrot, onion, celery, and cabbage.
Stir in the chopped parsley and
season with salt and pepper.

2 Heat the sesame oil in a saucepan
with a lid. Add the poppy seeds and
cover the pan. Cook over a medium-
high heat until the seeds start to
make a popping sound. Remove from
the heat and leave to cool.

3 Scatter the cashew nuts onto a
cookie sheet. Place them under a
medium-hot broiler and toast until
lightly browned, being careful not to
burn them. Leave to cool.

4 Add the vinegar to the oil and
poppy seeds, mix well, then pour over
the carrot mixture. Add the cooled
cashew nuts and toss together to coat
with the dressing. Garnish the salad
with sprigs of parsley and serve
immediately.

Gado Gado

This is a very well-known Indonesian salad of mixed
vegetables with a peanut dressing.

Serves 4
3^1/$_2$ ounces white cabbage, shredded
3^1/$_2$ ounces green beans, cut into 3
3^1/$_2$ ounces carrots, cut into matchsticks
3^1/$_2$ ounces cauliflower florets
3^1/$_2$ ounces bean sprouts
DRESSING
^{1}/$_2$ cup vegetable oil
1 cup unsalted peanuts
2 garlic cloves, crushed
1 small onion, finely chopped
^{1}/$_2$ tsp chili powder
^{1}/$_3$ tsp light brown sugar
2 cups water
juice of ^{1}/$_2$ lemon
salt
sliced scallions, to garnish

1 Cook the vegetables separately in
saucepans of salted, boiling water
for 4–5 minutes, drain well, and
leave to chill.

2 To make the dressing, heat the oil
in a skillet and fry the peanuts for
3–4 minutes, turning. Remove from
the pan with a slotted spoon and
leave to drain on absorbent paper
towels. Grind the peanuts in a
blender or crush with a rolling pin
until a fine mixture is formed.

3 Pour all but 1 tablespoon of oil
from the pan and fry the garlic and
onions for 1 minute. Add the chili
powder, sugar, a pinch of salt, and the
water and bring to a boil.

4 Stir in the peanuts. Reduce the heat
and simmer for 4–5 minutes until the
sauce thickens. Add the lemon juice
and leave to cool.

5 Arrange the vegetables in a serving
dish and spoon the peanut dressing
into the center. Garnish and serve.

COOK'S TIP

If necessary, you can prepare
the peanut dressing in advance
and then store it in the
refrigerator for up to 12 hours
before serving.

Salad with Garlic Yogurt Dressing

This is a very quick and refreshing salad using a whole range of colorful ingredients which make it look as good as it tastes.

Serves 4

2³/4 ounces cucumber,
cut into sticks

6 scallions, halved

2 tomatoes, seeded
and cut into eight

1 yellow bell pepper, cut into strips

2 celery sticks, cut into strips

4 radishes, quartered

2³/4 ounces arugula

1 tbsp chopped mint, to serve

DRESSING

2 tbsp lemon juice

1 garlic clove, crushed

²/3 cup natural yogurt

2 tbsp olive oil

salt and pepper

1 Mix the cucumber, scallions, tomatoes, bell pepper, celery, radishes, and arugula together in a large serving bowl.

2 To make the dressing, stir the lemon juice, garlic, yogurt, and oil together and season well.

3 Spoon the dressing over the salad and toss to mix. Sprinkle with chopped mint and serve.

COOK'S TIP

Do not toss the dressing into the salad until just before serving, otherwise it will turn soggy.

Three-Way Potato Salad

There's nothing to beat the flavor of new potatoes,
served just warm in a delicious dressing.

Serves 4
1 pound new potatoes, for each dressing
fresh herbs, to garnish
salt and pepper

LIGHT CURRY DRESSING

1 tbsp vegetable oil
1 tbsp medium curry paste
1 small onion, chopped
1 tbsp mango chutney, chopped
6 tbsp natural yogurt
3 tbsp light cream
2 tbsp mayonnaise
1 tbsp light cream, to garnish

VINAIGRETTE DRESSING

6 tbsp hazelnut oil
3 tbsp cider vinegar
1 tsp wholegrain mustard
1 tsp superfine sugar
few basil leaves, torn into shreds

PARSLEY, SCALLION, & SOUR CREAM DRESSING

$^2/_3$ cup sour cream
3 tbsp light mayonnaise
4 scallions, trimmed and chopped finely
1 tbsp chopped fresh parsley

1 To make the Light Curry Dressing, heat the vegetable oil in a skillet. Add the curry paste and onion and fry together, stirring frequently, until the onion is soft. Remove the pan from the heat and leave to cool slightly.

2 Mix together the mango chutney, yogurt, cream, and mayonnaise. Add the curry mixture and blend together. Season with salt and pepper.

3 To make the Vinaigrette Dressing, whisk the hazelnut oil, cider vinegar, mustard, sugar, and basil together in a small jug or bowl. Season with salt and pepper to taste.

4 To make the Parsley, Scallion, and Sour Cream Dressing, combine all the ingredients, mixing well. Season with salt and pepper.

5 Cook the potatoes in a pan of lightly salted, boiling water until just tender. Drain and leave to cool for 5 minutes. Add the chosen dressing, tossing to coat. Serve, garnished with fresh herbs, spooning a little light cream on to the potatoes if you have used the curry dressing.

Bean, Avocado, & Tomato Salad

This is a colorful salad with a Mexican theme, using beans, tomatoes, and avocado.
The chili dressing adds a little kick.

Serves 4
lollo rosso lettuce
2 ripe avocados
2 tsp lemon juice
4 medium tomatoes
1 onion
2 cups mixed canned beans, drained

DRESSING
4 tbsp olive oil
drop of chili oil
2 tbsp garlic wine vinegar
pinch of superfine sugar
pinch of chili powder
1 tbsp chopped parsley

1 Line a serving bowl with the lettuce. Thinly slice the avocados and sprinkle with lemon juice.

2 Thinly slice the tomato and onion. Arrange the avocado, tomatoes, and onion around the salad bowl, leaving a space in the center.

3 Spoon the beans into the center of the salad and whisk the dressing ingredients together. Pour the dressing over the salad and serve.

COOK'S TIP

The lemon juice is sprinkled onto the avocados to prevent discoloration when in contact with the air. For this reason the salad should be prepared, assembled, and served quite quickly.

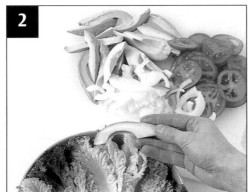

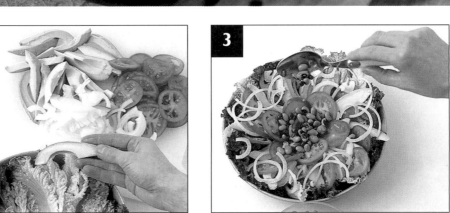

Broiled Vegetables with Mustard Dressing

The vegetables for this dish are best prepared well
in advance and chilled before serving.

Serves 4

1 zucchini, sliced
1 yellow bell pepper, sliced
1 eggplant, sliced
1 fennel bulb, cut into eight
1 red onion, cut into eight
16 cherry tomatoes
3 tbsp olive oil
1 garlic clove, crushed
fresh rosemary sprigs, to garnish

DRESSING

4 tbsp olive oil
2 tbsp balsamic vinegar
2 tsp chopped rosemary
1 tsp Dijon mustard
1 tsp clear honey
2 tsp lemon juice

1 Put all of the vegetables except for the cherry tomatoes onto a cookie sheet.

2 Mix the oil and garlic and brush over the vegetables. Cook under a medium-hot broiler for 10 minutes until tender and beginning to char. Leave to cool. Spoon the vegetables into a serving bowl.

3 Mix the dressing ingredients and pour over the vegetables. Cover and chill for 1 hour. Garnish and serve.

COOK'S TIP

This dish could also be served warm—heat the dressing in a pan and then toss into the vegetables.

Red Cabbage & Pear Salad

Red cabbage is much underused—it is a colorful and tasty ingredient
which is perfect with fruits, such as pears or apples.

Serves 4

12 ounces red cabbage,
finely shredded

2 Conference pears,
thinly sliced

4 scallions, sliced

1 carrot, grated

fresh chives, to garnish

lollo biondo leaves, to serve

DRESSING

4 tbsp pear juice

1 tsp wholegrain mustard

3 tbsp olive oil

1 tbsp garlic wine vinegar

1 tbsp chopped chives

1 Toss the cabbage, pears, and
scallions together.

2 Line a serving dish with lettuce
leaves and spoon the cabbage and
pear mixture into the center.

3 Sprinkle the carrot into the center
of the cabbage to form a domed pile.

4 To make the dressing, mix the pear
juice, mustard, oil, wine vinegar, and
chives together. Pour the dressing
over the salad, garnish, and serve
immediately.

COOK'S TIP

Mix the salad just before serving
to prevent the color from the red
cabbage bleeding into the
other ingredients.

Three Bean Salad

Fresh thin green beans are combined with soya beans and
red kidney beans in a chive and tomato dressing to make a tasty salad.

Serves 4–6
3 tbsp olive oil
1 tbsp lemon juice
1 tbsp tomato paste
1 tbsp light malt vinegar
1 tbsp chopped fresh chives
6 ounces thin green beans
14 ounce can soya beans, rinsed and drained
14 ounce can red kidney beans, rinsed and drained
2 tomatoes, chopped
4 scallions, trimmed and chopped
4½ ounces Feta cheese, cut into cubes
salt and pepper
mixed salad greens, to serve
chopped fresh chives, to garnish

1 Put the olive oil, lemon juice,
tomato paste, vinegar, and chives into
a large bowl and whisk together until
thoroughly combined.

2 Cook the thin green beans in a
little boiling, lightly salted water until
just cooked, about 4–5 minutes.
Drain, refresh under cold running
water, and drain again. Pat dry with
paper towels.

COOK'S VARIATION

Try navy beans or black-eye peas
instead of the soya beans and
red kidney beans.

3 Add the green beans, soya beans,
and red kidney beans to the dressing,
stirring to mix.

4 Add the tomatoes, scallions, and
Feta cheese to the bean mixture,
tossing gently to coat in the dressing.

Season well with salt and pepper
to taste.

5 Arrange the mixed salad leaves on
4 serving plates. Transfer the bean
salad to serving plates and garnish
with chopped chives.

Marinated Vegetable Salad

Lightly steamed vegetables taste superb served slightly warm in a marinade
of olive oil, white wine, vinegar, and fresh herbs.

Serves 4-6
6 ounces baby carrots, trimmed
2 celery hearts, cut into 4 pieces
4½ ounces sugar snap peas or snow peas
1 fennel bulb, sliced
6 ounces small asparagus spears
1½ tbsp sunflower seeds
sprigs of fresh dill, to garnish

DRESSING

4 tbsp olive oil
4 tbsp dry white wine
2 tbsp white wine vinegar
1 tbsp chopped fresh dill
1 tbsp chopped fresh parsley
salt and pepper

1 Steam the carrots, celery, sugar snap peas or snow peas, fennel, and asparagus over a pan of gently boiling water until just tender. It is important that they retain a little "bite."

2 Meanwhile, make the dressing. Mix together the olive oil, white wine, white wine vinegar, and chopped herbs. Season well with salt and pepper.

3 When the vegetables are cooked, transfer to a serving dish and pour over the dressing at once. The hot vegetables will absorb the flavor of the dressing as they cool.

4 Scatter the sunflower seeds onto a cookie sheet and toast them under a preheated broiler until lightly browned. Sprinkle them over the vegetables.

5 Serve the salad while the vegetables are still slightly warm, garnished with sprigs of fresh dill.

COOK'S VARIATION

Sesame seeds or pine nuts can be used instead of sunflower seeds for sprinkling over the vegetables.

Goat Cheese with Walnuts in Oil & Vinegar Dressing

This delicious salad combines soft goat cheese with walnut halves, served on a bed of mixed salad greens.

Serves 4
1 cup walnut halves
mixed salad greens
4¹/₂ ounces soft goat cheese
snipped fresh chives, to garnish
DRESSING
6 tbsp walnut oil
3 tbsp white wine vinegar
1 tbsp clear honey
1 tsp Dijon mustard
pinch of ground ginger
salt and pepper

1 To make the dressing, whisk together the walnut oil, wine vinegar, honey, mustard, and ginger in a small saucepan. Season to taste.

2 Heat the dressing gently, stirring occasionally, until warm. Add the walnut halves and continue to heat for 3–4 minutes.

3 Arrange the salad leaves on 4 serving plates and place spoonfuls of goat cheese on top. Lift the walnut halves from the dressing with a perforated spoon, and scatter them over the salad.

4 Transfer the warm dressing to a small jug. Sprinkle chives over the salad and serve with the dressing.

COOK'S VARIATION

Use hazelnut oil and hazelnuts rather than walnut oil and walnuts.

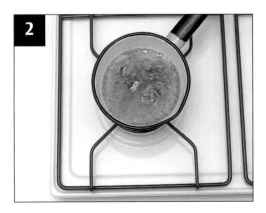

Barbecued Haloumi with Tomato & Red Onion Salad

Haloumi is a type of Cypriot cheese which remains firm and takes on a marvellous flavor when quickly barbecued.

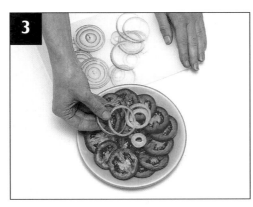

Serves 4
1 pound 2 ounces Haloumi, thickly sliced
fresh basil leaves, to garnish

ORANGE MARINADE

¹/₂ orange
¹/₄ cup olive oil
2 tbsp dry white wine
2 tbsp white wine vinegar
¹/₂ tbsp snipped fresh chives
¹/₂ tbsp chopped fresh marjoram
salt and pepper

SALAD

9 ounces plum tomatoes
1 small red onion
4 tbsp olive oil
2 tbsp cider vinegar
1 tsp lemon juice
pinch of ground coriander
2 tsp chopped fresh cilantro
salt and pepper

1 To make the orange marinade, remove the rind from the orange with a zester, or grate it finely, then squeeze the juice. Mix the orange rind and juice with all the remaining ingredients in a small bowl, whisking together to combine.

2 Place the Haloumi in a shallow dish and pour the marinade over. Cover and chill for at least 30 minutes.

3 To make the salad, slice the tomatoes and arrange them on a serving plate. Slice the onion thinly and scatter over the tomatoes.

4 Whisk together the olive oil, vinegar, lemon juice, ground coriander, and fresh cilantro. Season to taste with salt and pepper, then drizzle the dressing over the tomatoes and onions. Cover and chill.

5 Drain the marinade from the Haloumi. Cook the Haloumi over a hot barbecue for 2 minutes, turning once.

6 Transfer to plates, garnish, and serve with the salad.

Desserts

Vegetarian or not, confirmed pudding lovers feel disappointed if there isn't a tempting dessert to finish off a good meal. Desserts help satisfy a deep-seated desire for something sweet, but they are often loaded with fat and sugar which are notorious for piling on the calories.

The recipes in this chapter offer the ideal solution. They are light but full of flavor, so you can still enjoy that sweet treat without the bulging waistline and distended feeling at the end of a meal. This is particularly important after a vegetarian meal as the food can often be quite filling.

A lot of the recipes are based on fruit, which is the perfect ingredient for healthy desserts that are every bit as tempting as those based on lavish amounts of cream and butter. We've also included one or two indulgences such as Boston Chocolate Pie and Chocolate Chip Ice Cream.

Berry Cheesecake

Use a mixture of berries, such as blueberries, blackberries, raspberries, and strawberries, for a really fruity cheesecake.

Serves 8
BASE
6 tbsp vegetarian margarine
6 ounces oatmeal biscuits
$^3/_4$ cup shredded coconut
TOPPING
1$^1/_2$ tsp gelozone
9 tbsp cold water
$^1/_2$ cup evaporated milk
1 egg
6 tbsp light brown sugar
2 cups soft cream cheese
1$^3/_4$ cups mixed berries
2 tbsp clear honey

5 Remove the cheesecake from the pan and transfer to a serving plate. Arrange the remaining berries on top of the cheesecake and drizzle the honey over the top. Serve.

COOK'S TIP

Warm the honey slightly to make it runnier and easier to drizzle.

1 Put the margarine in a saucepan and heat until melted. Put the biscuits in a food processor and blend until smooth or crush finely with a rolling pin. Stir into the margarine with the coconut. Press the mixture into a base-lined 8 inch spring-form pan and chill while preparing the filling.

2 To make the topping, sprinkle the gelozone over the water and stir to dissolve. Bring to a boil and boil for 2 minutes. Let cool slightly.

3 Put the milk, egg, sugar, and soft cream cheese in a bowl and beat until smooth. Stir in $^1/_4$ cup of the berries. Stir in the gelozone in a stream, stirring constantly.

4 Spoon the mixture onto the biscuit base and return to the refrigerator for 2 hours or until set.

Apricot Brûlée

Serve this delicious dessert with crisp-baked meringues
for an extra-special occasion.

Serves 4
4¹⁄₂ ounces unsulphured dried apricots
²⁄₃ cup orange juice
4 egg yolks
2 tbsp superfine sugar
²⁄₃ cup natural yogurt
²⁄₃ cup heavy cream
1 tsp vanilla extract
¹⁄₂ cup demerara sugar
meringues, to serve (optional)

1 Place the apricots in a bowl. Pour the orange juice over the apricots and leave to soak for at least 1 hour. Pour into a small saucepan, bring slowly to a boil, and simmer for 20 minutes. Purée the apricot mixture in a blender or food processor, or chop very finely and push through a strainer.

2 In a bowl, beat together the egg yolks and sugar until the mixture is light and fluffy. Place the yogurt in a small pan, add the cream and vanilla, and bring to a boil over a low heat.

3 Gradually pour the yogurt mixture over the eggs, beating well after each addition, then transfer to the top of a double boiler, or place the bowl over a pan of simmering water. Stir until the custard thickens.

4 Divide the apricot mixture between 6 ramekins and spoon the custard on top. Cool, then leave to chill in the refrigerator.

5 Preheat the broiler to high. Sprinkle the demerara sugar over the custard and broil until the sugar caramelizes. Set aside to cool.

6 To serve the apricot brûlée, crack the hard caramel topping with the back of a tablespoon. Serve with the meringues, if using.

Cherry Pancakes

This dish can be made with either fresh pitted cherries or canned cherries for speed.

Serves 4
FILLING
14 ounce can pitted cherries, plus juice
1/2 tsp almond extract
1/2 tsp mixed spice
2 tbsp cornstarch
PANCAKES
3/4 cup all-purpose flour
pinch of salt
2 tbsp chopped mint
1 egg
1 1/4 cups milk
vegetable oil, for frying
confectioners' sugar and toasted slivered almonds, to decorate

1 Put the cherries and 1 1/4 cups of the juice in a pan with the almond extract and mixed spice. Stir in the cornstarch and bring to a boil, stirring until thickened and clear. Set aside.

2 To make the pancakes, sieve the flour into a bowl with the salt. Add the chopped mint and make a well in the center. Gradually beat in the egg and milk to make a smooth batter.

3 Heat 1 tablespoon of oil in a 7 inch skillet; pour off the oil when hot. Add just enough batter to coat the base of the skillet and cook for 1–2 minutes or until the underside is cooked. Flip the pancake over and cook for 1 minute. Remove from the skillet and keep warm. Heat 1 tablespoon of the oil in the skillet again and repeat to use up all the batter.

4 Spoon a quarter of the cherry filling onto a quarter of each pancake and fold the pancake into a cone shape. Dust with confectioners' sugar and sprinkle the slivered almonds over the top. Serve.

COOK'S VARIATION

Use other fillings, such as gooseberries or blackberries, as an alternative to the cherries.

Chocolate Chip Ice Cream

This frozen dessert offers the best of both worlds—delicious cookies and a rich dairy-flavored ice cream.

Serves 6
1¹/₄ cups milk
1 vanilla pod
2 eggs
2 egg yolks
¹/₄ cup superfine sugar
1¹/₄ cups natural yogurt
4¹/₂ ounces chocolate chip cookies, broken into small pieces

6 Remove the ice cream from the freezer every hour and beat vigorously to prevent ice crystals forming. Alternatively, freeze the mixture in an ice-cream maker, following the manufacturer's instructions.

7 To serve the chocolate chip ice cream, transfer it to the main part of the refrigerator for 1 hour to soften slightly—this will make it much easier for serving. Serve in scoops.

1 Pour the milk into a small pan, add the vanilla pod, and bring slowly to a boil. Remove the pan from the heat, cover, and leave to cool.

2 Beat the eggs and egg yolks in a double boiler, or in a bowl set over a pan of simmering water. Add the sugar and continue beating until the mixture is pale and creamy.

3 Reheat the milk to simmering point and strain it over the egg mixture. Stir continuously until the custard is thick enough to coat the back of a spoon. Remove the custard from the heat and stand the pan or bowl in cold water to prevent any further cooking. Wash and dry the vanilla pod for future use.

4 Stir the yogurt into the cooled custard and beat until it is well blended. When the mixture is thoroughly cold, stir in the broken chocolate chip cookies.

5 Transfer the mixture to a chilled metal cake pan or plastic container, cover, and freeze for 4 hours.

Raspberry Fool

This dish is very easy to make and can be made in advance
and stored in the refrigerator.

Serves 4
10½ ounces fresh raspberries
¼ cup confectioners' sugar
½ tsp vanilla extract
1¼ cups crème fraîche, plus extra to decorate
2 egg whites
raspberries and lemon balm leaves, to decorate

1 Put the raspberries and confectioners' sugar in a food processor or blender and blend until smooth.

2 Put the vanilla extract and crème fraîche (reserving 1 tablespoon per portion for decorating) in a bowl and stir in the raspberry mixture.

3 Whisk the egg whites in a separate mixing bowl until stiff peaks form and fold into the raspberry mixture until fully incorporated.

4 Spoon the raspberry fool into serving dishes and chill for at least 1 hour. Decorate and serve.

COOK'S VARIATION

This recipe is also delicious made with strawberries or blackberries.

Steamed Coffee Sponge & Sauce

This sponge pudding is very light and is delicious
with a coffee or chocolate sauce.

Serves 4
2 tbsp vegetarian margarine
2 tbsp soft brown sugar
2 eggs
$1/3$ cup all-purpose flour
$3/4$ tsp baking powder
6 tbsp milk
1 tsp coffee extract
SAUCE
$1^1/4$ cups milk
1 tbsp soft brown sugar
1 tsp cocoa powder
2 tbsp cornstarch

1 Lightly grease a 1 pint heatproof
pudding basin. Cream the margarine
and sugar until light and fluffy and
beat in the eggs.

2 Gradually stir in the flour and
baking powder and then the milk
and coffee extract to make a
smooth batter.

3 Spoon the mixture into the
prepared pudding basin and cover
with a pleated piece of greaseproof
paper and then a pleated piece of foil,
securing around the bowl with a piece
of string. Place in a steamer or large
pan and half fill with boiling water.
Cover and steam for 1–1½ hours or
until cooked through.

4 To make the sauce, put the milk,
sugar, and cocoa powder in a
saucepan and heat until the sugar
dissolves. Blend the cornstarch with
4 tablespoons of cold water to make a
paste and stir into the mixture in the
saucepan. Bring to a boil, stirring until
thickened. Cook over a gentle heat for
1 minute.

5 Turn the pudding out onto a serving
plate and spoon the sauce over the
top. Serve.

COOK'S TIP

The pudding is covered with pleated
paper and foil to allow it to rise.
The foil will react with the steam
and must therefore not be placed
directly against the pudding.

Lemon & Lime Syllabub

This dessert is rich but absolutely delicious. It is not, however, for the
calorie conscious as it contains a high proportion of cream,
but it's well worth blowing the diet for!

Serves 4
¹/₄ cup superfine sugar
grated zest and juice of 1 small lemon
grated zest and juice of 1 small lime
4 tbsp Marsala or medium sherry
1¹/₄ cups heavy cream
lime and lemon zest, to decorate

1 Put the sugar, fruit juices and zest, and sherry in a bowl, mix well, and leave to infuse for 2 hours.

2 Add the cream to the mixture and whisk until it just holds its shape.

3 Spoon the mixture into 4 tall serving glasses and chill in the refrigerator for 2 hours before decorating and serving.

COOK'S TIP

Serve with almond biscuits or uncoated florentines. Do not overwhip the cream when adding to the lemon and lime mixture as it may curdle.

Warm Currants in Cassis

Crème de cassis is a blackcurrant-based liqueur which comes
from France and is an excellent flavoring for fruit dishes.

Serves 4
12 ounces blackcurrants
9 ounces redcurrants
4 tbsp superfine sugar
grated rind and juice of 1 orange
2 tsp arrowroot
2 tbsp crème de cassis
fresh mint leaves, to decorate
whipped cream, to serve

1 Using a fork, strip the currants
from their stalks and place in a
saucepan.

2 Add the sugar and orange rind and
juice, and heat gently until the sugar
has dissolved. Bring to a boil and
simmer gently for 5 minutes.

3 Strain the currants and place in a
bowl. Return the juice to the pan.

4 Blend the arrowroot with a little
water. Mix the arrowroot into the
juice then boil until thickened.

5 Leave to cool slightly, then stir in
the cassis.

6 Serve in individual dishes with
whipped cream.

Cherry Clafoutis

This is a hot dessert that is simple and quick to put together. Try the batter with other fruits—apricots and plums are particularly delicious.

Serves 6
1 cup all-purpose flour
4 eggs, lightly beaten
2 tbsp superfine sugar
pinch of salt
2½ cups milk
butter, for greasing
1 pound 2 ounces black cherries, fresh or canned, pitted
3 tbsp brandy
1 tbsp sugar, to decorate

1 Sift the flour into a large bowl. Make a well in the center and add the eggs, sugar, and salt. Draw in the flour from around the edges and whisk.

2 Pour in the milk and whisk the batter thoroughly until very smooth.

3 Lightly grease a 3 pint ovenproof serving dish and pour in half of the batter.

4 Spoon in the cherries and pour the remaining batter over the top. Sprinkle the brandy over the batter.

5 Bake in a preheated oven at 350°F for 40 minutes.

6 Remove from the oven and sprinkle with the sugar just before serving. Serve warm.

Fruit & Nut Loaf

This loaf is like a fruit bread which may be served warm or cold,
perhaps spread with a little vegetarian margarine or butter or topped with jam.

Makes 1 loaf

1³/₄ cups white bread flour,
plus extra for dusting

¹/₂ tsp salt

1 tbsp vegetarian margarine,
plus extra for greasing

2 tbsp soft light
brown sugar

²/₃ cup golden raisins

1³/₄ ounces no-need-to-soak dried
apricots, chopped

¹/₂ cup chopped hazelnuts

2 tsp easy-blend dried yeast

6 tbsp orange juice

6 tbsp natural yogurt

2 tbsp sieved apricot jam

1 Sieve the flour and salt into a
mixing bowl. Rub in the margarine
and stir in the sugar, golden raisins,
apricots, nuts, and yeast.

2 Warm the orange juice in a
saucepan but do not allow to boil.

3 Stir the warm orange juice into
the flour mixture with the yogurt
and bring the mixture together to
form a dough.

4 Knead the dough on a lightly
floured surface for 5 minutes until
smooth and elastic. Shape into a
round and place on a lightly greased
cookie sheet. Cover with a clean dish
cloth and leave to rise in a warm place
until doubled in size.

5 Cook the loaf in a preheated oven
at 425°F for 35–40 minutes until
cooked through. Transfer to a cooling
rack and brush with the apricot jam.
Leave to cool before serving.

COOK'S TIP

To test if the loaf is cooked
through—tap the base and if it
sounds hollow, it's cooked.

Cinnamon Pears with Maple & Ricotta Cream

These spicy yet sweet pears are accompanied by a delicious melt-in-the-mouth cream, which is relatively low in fat.

Serves 4
1 lemon
4 firm ripe pears
1 cinnamon stick, broken in half
1¼ cups dry cider or unsweetened apple juice
fresh mint leaves, to decorate

MAPLE RICOTTA CREAM

½ cup medium-fat Ricotta
½ cup low-fat natural fromage frais
½ tsp ground cinnamon
½ tsp grated lemon rind
1 tbsp maple syrup
grated lemon rind, to decorate

1 Using a vegetable peeler, remove the rind from the lemon and place in a non-stick skillet. Squeeze the lemon and pour the juice into a shallow bowl.

2 Peel, halve, and core the pears. Place in a bowl and toss in the lemon juice to prevent discoloration. Add to the skillet and pour over the lemon juice remaining in the bowl.

3 Add the cinnamon stick and cider or apple juice. Bring to a boil, then lower the heat, and simmer for 10 minutes. Remove the pears using a slotted spoon, reserving the cooking juice.

4 Put the pears in a warm heatproof serving dish, cover with foil, and keep warm in a preheated oven at 225°F.

5 Return the pan to the heat, bring to a boil, then simmer for 8–10 minutes until reduced by half. Spoon the syrup over the pears.

6 To make the maple Ricotta cream, mix together all the ingredients. Decorate with lemon rind and serve with the pears.

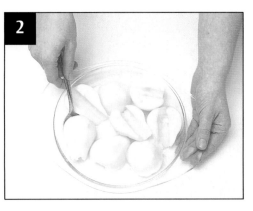

Blackberry, Apple, & Fresh Fig Compôte

Elderflower cordial is used in the syrup for this refreshing fruit compôte, giving it a delightfully summery flavor.

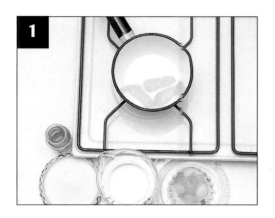  

Serves 4
1 lemon
¹/₄ cup superfine sugar
4 tbsp elderflower cordial
1¹/₄ cups water
4 eating apples
2 cups blackberries
2 fresh figs
SAUCE
²/₃ cup thick natural yogurt
2 tbsp clear honey

1 Pare the rind from the lemon, using a potato peeler. Squeeze the juice. Put the lemon rind and juice into a saucepan with the sugar, elderflower cordial, and water. Heat gently and simmer, uncovered, for 10 minutes.

2 Core and slice the apples, then add them to the saucepan. Simmer gently for 4–5 minutes or until just tender. Leave to cool.

3 Transfer the apples and syrup to a serving bowl and add the blackberries. Slice the figs and add to the bowl, stirring gently to mix. Cover and chill until ready to serve.

4 To make the sauce, spoon the yogurt into a small serving bowl and drizzle the honey over the top. Cover and chill before serving.

Fall Fruit Bread Pudding

This is like a summer pudding, but it uses fruits which appear later in the year, such as apples, pears, and blackberries, as a succulent filling.

Serves 8
4 cups mixed blackberries, chopped apples, chopped pears
$^3/_4$ cup sugar
1 tsp cinnamon
8 ounces white bread, thinly sliced, crusts removed

1 Place the fruit in a large saucepan with the sugar, cinnamon, and scant $^1/_2$ cup of water, stir, and bring to a boil. Reduce the heat and simmer for 5–10 minutes so that the fruits soften but still hold their shape.

2 Meanwhile, line the base and sides of a 1$^1/_2$ pint pudding basin with the bread slices, ensuring that there are no gaps between the pieces of bread.

3 Spoon the fruit into the center of the bread-lined bowl and cover the fruit with the remaining bread.

4 Place a saucer on top of the bread and weight it down. Leave to chill in the refrigerator overnight.

5 Turn the pudding out onto a serving plate and serve immediately.

COOK'S TIP

Stand the pudding on a plate when chilling to catch any juices that run down the sides of the basin.

Green Fruit Salad with Mint & Lemon Syrup

This delightful fresh fruit salad is the perfect finale for a summer barbecue.
It has a lovely light syrup made with fresh mint and honey.

Serves 4

1 small Charentais or honeydew melon

2 green apples

2 kiwi fruit

4$^1/_2$ ounces seedless white grapes

fresh mint sprigs, to decorate

SYRUP

1 lemon

$^2/_3$ cup white wine

$^2/_3$ cup water

4 tbsp clear honey

few sprigs of fresh mint

1 To make the syrup, pare the rind from the lemon, using a potato peeler.

2 Put the lemon rind in a saucepan with the wine, water, and honey. Bring to a boil, then simmer gently for 10 minutes. Remove from the heat. Add the sprigs of mint and leave to cool.

3 Slice the melon in half and scoop out the seeds. Using a melon baller or a teaspoon, scoop out melon balls.

4 Core and chop the apples. Peel and slice the kiwi fruit.

5 Strain the cooled syrup into a serving bowl, removing and reserving the lemon rind, and discarding the mint sprigs. Add the apple, grapes, kiwi, and melon. Stir gently to mix.

6 Decorate with sprigs of fresh mint and some of the reserved lemon rind and serve.

Chocolate Mousse

This is a light and fluffy, but fruity-tasting mousse which
is delicious with a fresh fruit sauce.

Serves 8
3¹/₂ ounces dark chocolate, melted
1¹/₄ cups natural yogurt
²/₃ cup Quark
4 tbsp superfine sugar
1 tbsp orange juice
1 tbsp brandy
1¹/₂ tsp gelozone
9 tbsp cold water
2 large egg whites
coarsely grated dark and white chocolate and orange zest, to decorate

1 Put the chocolate, yogurt, Quark, sugar, orange juice, and brandy in a food processor and blend for 30 seconds. Transfer to a mixing bowl.

2 Sprinkle the gelozone over the water and stir until dissolved. Bring to a boil for 2 minutes. Cool slightly, then stir into the chocolate mixture.

3 Whisk the egg whites until peaking and fold into the chocolate mixture.

4 Line a 1¹/₂ pint loaf pan with plastic wrap. Spoon the mousse into the pan. Chill for 2 hours until set. Turn the mousse out onto a plate, decorate, and serve.

COOK'S TIP

For a quick fruit sauce, blend a can of mandarin segments in natural juice in a food processor and press through a sieve. Stir in 1 tbsp clear honey and serve with the mousse.

Boston Chocolate Pie

This lighter version of the popular chocolate cream pie
is made with yogurt and crème fraîche.

Serves 6
9 ounces shortcrust pastry
9 ounces dark chocolate
2/3 cup crème fraîche
FILLING
3 eggs
1/2 cup superfine sugar
1/2 cup flour, plus extra for dusting
1 tbsp confectioners' sugar, plus extra to decorate
pinch of salt
1 tsp vanilla extract
13/4 cups milk
2/3 cup natural yogurt
51/2 ounces dark chocolate, broken into pieces
2 tbsp kirsch

1 Roll out the pastry and use to line a 9 inch loose-bottomed flan pan. Prick the base with a fork, line with baking parchment, fill with baking beans, and bake blind in a preheated oven at 400°F for 20 minutes. Remove the beans and parchment and return to the oven for 5 minutes. Cool on a wire rack.

2 To make the Chocolate Caraque, melt the chocolate in a heatproof bowl set over a pan of simmering water. Spread onto a cool surface with a spatula. When cool, scrape it into curls by drawing a sharp knife firmly across the surface.

3 To make the filling, beat the eggs and sugar until fluffy. Sieve the flour,

confectioners' sugar and salt over the beaten eggs and stir until blended. Stir in the vanilla extract. Put the milk and yogurt in a small pan, bring slowly to a boil, then strain into the egg mixture. Pour into the top of a double boiler, or a bowl set over a pan of simmering water, and stir until thick enough to coat the back of a spoon. Melt the chocolate and kirsch over a low heat.

When it has melted, stir into the custard. Remove the custard from the heat and stand the double boiler or bowl in cold water to prevent further cooking. Leave to cool.

4 Pour the chocolate filling into the pastry case. Spread the crème fraîche over the chocolate, and arrange the caraque on top.

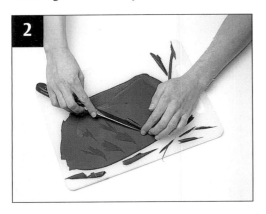

Fruit Brûlée

This is a cheat's brûlée, in that yogurt is used to cover a base of fruit, before being sprinkled with sugar and broiled.

Serves 4
4 plums, stoned and sliced
2 cooking apples, peeled and sliced
1 tsp ground ginger
2½ cups Greek-style yogurt
2 tbsp confectioners' sugar, sieved
1 tsp almond extract
⅓ cup demerara sugar

1 Put the plums and apples in a saucepan with 2 tablespoons of water and cook for 7–10 minutes until tender but not mushy. Leave to cool, then stir in the ginger. Using a slotted spoon, spoon the mixture into the base of a shallow serving dish.

2 Mix the yogurt, confectioners' sugar, and almond extract together and spoon onto the fruit.

3 Sprinkle the demerara sugar over the top of the yogurt and cook under a hot broiler for 3–4 minutes or until the sugar has dissolved and formed a crust. Chill in the refrigerator for 1 hour and serve.

COOK'S TIP

Use any variety of fruit, such as mixed berries or mango pieces, for this dessert, but do not poach them.

Chocolate & Bean Curd Cheesecake

This cheesecake takes a little time to prepare and cook but is well worth the effort. It is quite rich and is good served or decorated with a little fresh fruit, such as sliced strawberries.

Serves 12
³/₄ cup all-purpose flour
³/₄ cup ground almonds
³/₄ cup demerara sugar
10 tbsp vegetarian margarine
1¹/₂ pounds firm bean curd
³/₄ cup vegetable oil
¹/₂ cup orange juice
³/₄ cup brandy
6 tbsp cocoa powder,
plus extra to decorate
2 tsp almond extract
confectioners' sugar and Cape
gooseberries, to decorate

1 Put the flour, ground almonds, and 1 tablespoon of the sugar in a bowl and mix well. Rub the margarine into the mixture to form a dough.

2 Lightly grease and line the base of a 9 inch spring-form pan. Press the dough into the base of the pan to cover.

3 Roughly chop the bean curd and put in a food processor with all of the remaining ingredients and blend until smooth and creamy. Pour over the base in the pan and cook in a preheated oven at 325°F for 1–1¹/₄ hours or until set.

4 Leave to cool in the pan for 5 minutes, then remove from the pan, and chill in the refrigerator. Dust with confectioners' sugar and cocoa powder. Decorate and serve.

Pear Cake

This is a really moist cake, flavored with chopped pears and cinnamon.

Serves 12
4 pears, peeled and cored
vegetarian margarine, for greasing
2 tbsp water
1½ cups all-purpose flour
2 tsp baking powder
½ cup soft light brown sugar
4 tbsp milk
2 tbsp clear honey, plus extra to drizzle
2 tsp ground cinnamon
2 egg whites

1 Grease and line the base of an 8 inch cake pan.

2 Put 1 pear in a food processor with the water and blend until almost smooth. Transfer to a mixing bowl.

3 Sieve in the flour and baking powder. Beat in the sugar, milk, honey, and cinnamon and mix well.

4 Chop all but one of the remaining pears and add to the mixture.

5 Whisk the egg whites until stiff peaks form and gently fold into the mixture until fully incorporated.

6 Slice the remaining pear and arrange in a fan pattern on the base of the pan.

7 Spoon the cake mixture into the pan and cook in a preheated oven at 300°F for 1¼–1½ hours or until cooked through.

8 Remove the cake from the oven and leave to cool in the pan for 10 minutes.

9 Turn the cake out onto a wire cooling rack and drizzle with honey. Leave to cool completely, then cut into slices to serve.

COOK'S TIP

To test if the cake is cooked through, insert a skewer into the center—if it comes out clean the cake is cooked. If not, return the cake to the oven and test at frequent intervals.

Banana & Mango Tart

Bananas and mangoes are a great combination of colors and flavors, especially when topped with toasted coconut chips.

Serves 8
PASTRY
8 inch baked pastry case
FILLING
2 small ripe bananas
1 mango, sliced
3$\frac{1}{2}$ tbsp cornstarch
6 tbsp demerara sugar
1$\frac{1}{4}$ cups soya milk
$\frac{2}{3}$ cup coconut milk
1 tsp vanilla extract
toasted coconut chips, to decorate

1 Slice the bananas and arrange half in the baked pastry case with half of the mango pieces.

2 Put the cornstarch and sugar in a saucepan and mix together. Slowly stir in the soya and coconut milks until combined and cook over a low heat, stirring until the mixture thickens. Stir in the vanilla extract. Pour the mixture over the fruit.

3 Top with the remaining fruit and toasted coconut chips. Chill in the refrigerator for 1 hour before serving.

COOK'S TIP

Coconut chips are available in some supermarkets and most health food shops. It is worth using them as they look much more attractive and are not as sweet as shredded coconut.

Chocolate Fudge Pudding

This pudding has a hidden surprise when cooked as it separates
to give a rich chocolate sauce at the bottom of the dish.

Serves 4

4 tbsp vegetarian margarine,
plus extra for greasing

6 tbsp soft light brown sugar

2 eggs, beaten

1$\frac{1}{4}$ cups milk

1$\frac{3}{4}$ ounces chopped walnuts

$\frac{1}{4}$ cup all-purpose flour

2 tbsp cocoa powder

confectioners' sugar and cocoa powder,
to dust

1 Lightly grease a 1$\frac{3}{4}$ pint ovenproof
dish with a little margarine.

2 Cream the margarine and sugar
until fluffy and beat in the eggs.

3 Gradually stir in the milk and add
the walnuts.

4 Sieve the flour and cocoa powder
into the mixture and fold in gently
until well mixed.

5 Spoon the mixture into the dish
and cook in a preheated oven at
350°F for 35–40 minutes or until the
sponge is cooked. Dust with
confectioners' sugar and cocoa
powder and serve.

COOK'S VARIATION

Add 1–2 tbsp brandy or rum to the
mixture for a slightly alcoholic
pudding, or 1–2 tbsp orange juice
for a child-friendly version.

Passion Cake

Decorating this moist, rich carrot cake with sugared flowers lifts
it into the celebration class. It is a perfect choice for Easter.

Serves 8-10

²/₃ cup corn oil

³/₄ cup golden superfine sugar

4 tbsp natural yogurt

3 eggs, plus 1 extra yolk

1 tsp vanilla extract

1 cup walnut pieces,
chopped

6 ounces carrots, grated

1 banana, mashed

1¹/₂ cups all-purpose flour

¹/₂ cup fine oatmeal

1 tsp baking soda

1 tsp baking powder

1 tsp ground cinnamon

¹/₂ tsp salt

FROSTING

generous ¹/₂ cup low-fat
soft cheese

4 tbsp natural yogurt

³/₄ cup confectioners' sugar

1 tsp grated lemon rind

2 tsp lemon juice

DECORATION

primroses and violets

1 egg white, lightly beaten

3 tbsp superfine sugar

1 Grease and line a 9 inch round cake
pan. Beat the oil, sugar, yogurt, eggs,
egg yolk, and vanilla. Beat in the
walnuts, carrot, and banana. Sift the
remaining ingredients and beat into
the mixture.

2 Pour the mixture into the pan and
level the surface. Bake in a preheated
oven at 350°F for 1¹/₂ hours or until
firm. Insert a skewer into the center: it
should come out clean. Cool in the
pan for 15 minutes, then transfer to
a wire rack.

3 To make the frosting, beat together
the cheese and yogurt. Sift in the
confectioners' sugar and stir in the
lemon rind and juice. Spread over the
top and sides of the cake. To prepare
the decoration, dip the flowers quickly
in the beaten egg white, then sprinkle
with superfine sugar to cover. Place
well apart on baking parchment. Leave
in a warm, dry place for several hours
until they are dry and crisp. Arrange
the flowers on top of the cake.

Index

Index compiled by Hilary Bird.